VISIONS OF GRACE

STORIES FROM SCRIPTURE

Edited by
ED GALLAGHER

Visions of Grace: Stories from Scripture

Published by Heritage Christian University Press

Copyright © 2019, 2021 by Ed Gallagher

Manufactured in the United States of America

Cataloging-in-Publication Data

Visions of grace: stories from Scripture/ edited by Ed Gallagher

p. cm.

Berean Study Series

Includes scripture index.

ISBN 978-1-956811-04-9 (pbk.) 978-1-956811-05-6 (ebook)

1. Grace. I. Gallagher, Edmon, L. editor. II. Title. III. Series.

234—dc20

Library of Congress Control Number: 2021920615

For information:
Heritage Christian University Press
3625 Helton Drive
PO Box HCU
Florence, AL 35630

www.hcu.edu

CONTENTS

BIBLE ABBREVIATIONS

Old Testament

Gen	Genesis
Exod	Exodus
Lev	Leviticus
Num	Numbers
Deut	Deuteronomy
Josh	Joshua
Judg	Judges
Ruth	Ruth
1–2 Sam	1–2 Samuel
1–2 Kgs	1–2 Kings
1–2 Chr	1–2 Chronicles
Ezra	Ezra
Neh	Nehemiah
Esth	Esther
Job	Job
Ps	Psalms
Prov	Proverbs

Eccl	Ecclesiastes
Song	Song of Solomon
Isa	Isaiah
Jer	Jeremiah
Lam	Lamentations
Ezek	Ezekiel
Dan	Daniel
Hos	Hosea
Joel	Joel
Amos	Amos
Obad	Obadiah
Jonah	Jonah
Mic	Micah
Nah	Nahum
Hab	Habakkuk
Zeph	Zephaniah
Hag	Haggai
Zech	Zechariah
Mal	Malachi

New Testament

Matt	Matthew
Mark	Mark
Luke	Luke
John	John
Acts	Acts
Rom	Romans
1–2 Cor	1–2 Corinthians
Gal	Galatians

Eph	Ephesians
Phil	Philippians
Col	Colossians
1–2 Thess	1–2 Thessalonians
1–2 Tim	1–2 Timothy
Titus	Titus
Phlm	Philemon
Heb	Hebrews
Jas	James
1–2 Pet	1–2 Peter
1–2–3 John	1–2–3 John
Jude	Jude
Rev	Revelation

INTRODUCTION
ED GALLAGHER

WHAT IS GRACE?

If you hear the word "grace," what do you think of? Well ... like Faith, Hope, and Charity, it can be a girl's name (Grace Kelly). Or it can refer to a prayer, especially before meals. (Who wants to say grace?) Sometimes it's a title for some sort of royalty or nobility (Your Grace). We sometimes use the word to talk about good manners (the social graces) or being favored by someone (in someone's good graces). We can use the word to describe a person's ability to handle tough situations. (She handled herself with grace.)

But what about the grace of God? What does that term signify? Unfortunately, the word "grace"—like "church" and "atonement"—might be one of those church-y words that people throw around and don't really understand, a word that does more to obscure than to reveal. Since the Bible is a book about God's grace, since that's really the point of this story, we need to take some time to under-

I

stand what we're talking about. I don't mean we should just get a good definition of "grace" and move on. We've put together these studies in order to help illuminate grace, to present a vision of it, or, rather, a series of visions.

But, definitions are helpful, so let's go there.

What is grace? If you ask this question at church, someone is going to say, "unmerited favor." Or how about this one—"grace is when God gives us what we don't deserve; mercy is when God doesn't give us what we do deserve."

These are helpful ways of thinking about God's grace toward us—unmerited favor, giving us what we don't deserve—but maybe we can press further.

We could talk about the English word. The word "grace" comes from French *grase*, which derives from Latin *gratia*. The word "grace" has been used in English since the thirteenth century. It appears in the KJV 170 times (39 of which are in the Old Testament). We've already seen that in English we've got all kinds of meanings for "grace," but we really care about what the words mean in the Bible. To figure that out, we're not going to rely on the English language but on the biblical languages of Greek and Hebrew.

The Greek word often translated "grace" (χάρις, *charis*) appears 155 times in the New Testament, exactly a hundred of which are in the thirteen letters of Paul. The word appears at least once in 23 New Testament writings (not Matthew, Mark, or 1 John, or 3 John). It also appears 132 times in the Greek Old Testament (the Septuagint or LXX).

The standard dictionary of New Testament Greek, edited about two decades ago by Fred Danker, provides these definitions for our word.[1]

1. a winning quality or attractiveness that invites a favorable reactions, graciousness, attractiveness, charm, winsomeness
2. a beneficent disposition toward someone, favor, grace, gracious care/help, goodwill
3. practical application of goodwill, (a sign of) favor, gracious deed/gift, benefaction
4. exceptional effect produced by generosity, favor
5. response to generosity or beneficence, thanks, gratitude

A recent book on "grace" in Paul simplifies these five definitions to three.[2]

- charm, delight. This meaning is common in the LXX. In the New Testament, see Luke 1:30; 2:52; Acts 7:46; 1 Peter 2:19–20; Colossians 4:6.
- the attitude of benevolence, or the favor or benefit given. This is the meaning we commonly associate with God.

- gratitude or thanksgiving. See 1 Corinthians 10:30; 2 Corinthians 9:11–12, 15.

These definitions apply to the single noun, but there are also other, related words, like χαρίζομαι (*charizomai*) and χάρισμα (charisma) and χαριτόω (*charitóō*), that all have something to do with favor or giving. If we free the concept of God's grace from this one domain of Greek words, we will want to talk about more terms and passages. For instance, the way Paul talks about "kindness" (χρηστότης; *chrēstotēs*; cf. Rom 2:4; 11:22) or "mercy" (ἔλεος, *eleos*; cf. Rom 15:29) or "blessing" (εὐλογία, *eulogia*; cf. Rom 15:29) or "love of people" (φιλανθρωπία, *philanthrōpia*; cf. Titus 3:4) illuminates in many ways the graciousness of God.[3]

In Hebrew, there are also a variety of terms associated with the concept of "grace," but the Hebrew word usually translated with "grace" is ḥen, or the verb "show favor," *ḥanan*, or the adjective "gracious," *ḥannun*. This is how God reveals himself to Moses on Sinai, when Moses asks to see God's glory and all God will show him is his "back."

The LORD, the LORD, a God merciful (רַחוּם , *raḥum*) and gracious (*ḥannun*), slow to anger, and abounding in steadfast love and faithfulness. (Exod 34:6)

That's just a quick review of some of the basic terminology in the Bible that will help you as you work your way through these lessons. We hope this vocabulary is helpful, but the vocabulary is not ultimately the point. What we really want to do is to show you pictures, visions, of our gracious God, and to motivate you to live graciously and gratefully in response to his bounteous gifts.

Endnotes

1. Frederick William Danker, ed., *A Greek-English Lexicon of the New Testament and Other Early Christian Literature*, 3rd ed. (Chicago: University of Chicago Press, 2000), 1079–80.

2. John M. G. *Barclay, Paul & the Gift* (Grand Rapids: Eerdmans 2015), 576–78.

3. See the brief discussion of these other terms in Barclay, *Paul & the Gift*, 575n1.

1. **THE DARKER THE SIN**
BILL BAGENTS

2 Peter 2:9

One Main Thing

God's grace is deeper, stronger, wider, and more surprising than we can imagine.

Introduction

Abraham's relative Lot is not a man we associate with grace. Generally, we remember him for bad choices that had tragic consequences. He made the selfish decision to take the well-watered plain of Jordan when Abram offered him his choice of grazing land (Gen 13:5–11). In one of the classic biblical examples of foreshadowing, "he pitched his tent even as far as Sodom" (Gen 13:12). Eventually he chose to live in Sodom (Gen 14:12). This led to his kidnapping and need for rescue by Abram and his servants (Gen 14:13–16). We understand why some view the kidnapping as a message to Lot that he was in the wrong place with the wrong people.

In a sense, Lot was rescued twice by his famous relative. As God informed Abraham of the coming destruction of the cities on the plain, Abraham interceded for those cities with the memorable question, "Would you also destroy the righteous with the wicked?" (Gen 18:22). Not even the Lord's minimum number of ten righteous people could be found. Still, God's angels warned Lot. Lot and two daughters were saved from the fire, but then comes one of the darkest episodes in all of Scripture (Gen 19:30–38). Two of the strongest enemies of ancient Israel originated from those sins. Yet, Lot ultimately stands as a stunning example of the surprising and persistent power of God's grace.

Going Deeper

In Genesis we note several examples of God's favor toward Lot. The Lord blessed both Abram and Lot materially. "… Their possessions were so great that they could not dwell together" (Gen 13:6). The Lord blessed Lot with a magnanimous relative in Abram (Gen 13:9–10). The Lord blessed Lot with safety within "exceedingly wicked" Sodom (Gen 13:13). The Lord blessed Lot with rescue of both his people and his property (Gen 14:16). The Lord blessed Lot and his wife with children, though we neither condone nor understand his proposed action toward those daughters in Genesis 19:8. Lot was blessed to be warned of the coming destruction of Sodom and to be urged out of the city (Gen 19:15–17). The text emphasizes that this was "the Lord being merciful to him." The Lord even granted Lot's request to escape to the city of Zoar, rather than fleeing directly to the mountains (Gen 19:17–22). Lot received grace after grace from God.

Between his dark episodes, Lot showed grace to others. He knew the danger that the two visitors to Sodom faced, so he "insisted strongly" that they enter the protection and hospitality of his house (Gen 19:1–3). He tried to protect them at personal risk (Gen 19:4–10). Lot cared for the lives of his sons-in-law, even to the point of lingering in Sodom to the cusp of the destruction (Gen 19:14–16).

While we appreciate biblical fairness and balance, the account of Lot in Genesis ends on a terrible note. If that were the end of the biblical account of Lot, we would never think of him as an example of God's grace.

The story of Lot resumes in 2 Peter 2, a chapter that stoutly announces God's certain judgment on false teachers and all who live in rebellion. But 2 Peter 2 also documents God's grace, His ability to save and His record of saving the righteous from the worst of circumstances. The evil world perished in the flood, but Noah, a preacher of righteousness, and seven others were saved (2 Pet 2:5). Sodom and Gomorrah were turned into ashes, but the Lord "delivered righteous Lot" (2 Pet 2:7). For emphasis, Lot is also called "a righteous man" and is described as one of "the godly" (2 Pet 2:8–9). Amazing!

The devil would love for us to misunderstand 2 Peter 2. He would love for us to ignore the whole of Scripture and conclude that Lot's sin never really mattered, that God arbitrarily closed His eyes (Isa 59:1–3, Rom 3:23 and 6:23). He would love for us to doubt the accuracy of Genesis or to view 2 Peter 2 as contradicting it. Short of that, he would love for us to declare the Bible beyond our understanding so that we would abandon its study.

How can 2 Peter 2:4–11 make sense in light of Lot's terrible actions recorded in Genesis? In a word, grace. God did not save Lot in his sin (Ezek 18:27–32). God saved Lot from his sin. Admittedly, the Genesis account does not document Lot's repentance. This stands as a great reminder of the brevity of Scripture. Numerous accounts don't end with the neat closure that we often prefer.

2 Peter 2 offers insight into the reasons Peter, by inspiration, could describe Lot as righteous. Lot was in Sodom, but he was not of Sodom (1 John 2:15–17). Lot did not stop recognizing sin as sin (2 Pet 2:7). Lot was tormented (troubled, grieved, afflicted) by the sins of those around him (2 Pet 2:8). And God delivered Lot from imminent destruction (2 Pet 2:9). In the end, Lot's

complicated and often lamentable story documents the triumph of God's grace in the life of a deeply flawed man. Lot's story is our story of the wondrous power of grace.

False applications are easy to list. "All's well that ends well. Despite all his sins, the biblical account of Lot ends on a positive note. His sins were really no big deal." Lot's bad choices put many good people in danger. Lot's sins cost him his wife, his sons-in-law, and his reputation. We have no clue how Lot's daughters could have ever looked him in the eye again. Without Lot's sins, would there have been any Ammonites or Moabites to afflict Israel throughout much of Old Testament history (Num 22–25; Judg 3, 10, 11; 2 Sam 12)? The story of Lot intersects Romans 6:1–2, "What shall we say then? Shall we continue in sin that grace may abound? Certainly not!"

A second false application is the popular claim: "See, I told you that righteousness is relative. All Lot needed to do to be called righteous was to be slightly less bad than the evil people around him." There is no biblical support for this view.

A third false application is the claim that the standard for righteousness changed in the New Testament. "Lot is never called 'righteous' in Genesis; he's only called righteous in the new era where grace covers every sin." That claim runs counter to the point of 2 Peter 2 and to the teaching of Jesus in Matthew 25.

What are the legitimate applications of Lot's story?

Grace means that no person need be defined by his worst acts and decisions. Just as David was forgiven of adultery, lies, and murder, Lot was forgiven by God. Just as Saul was forgiven for persecuting the church, we can be forgiven through grace (Rom 5:6–8). God remains better at forgiving than we are at sinning.

Even the most heinous and embarrassing of sins, from a human perspective, are not beyond the scope of God's grace. Lot's story helps us understand and appreciate 1 Corinthians 6:9–11. Lot helps us avoid the deadly error of declaring ourselves too evil for God to save.

Lot emphasizes a powerful lesson we first learn from Noah in Genesis 6. One person, one family, can choose righteousness even when the world around us rebels against God. We would never claim that this is easy, but we know that it is possible through God's grace (Titus 2:1–14).

Lot reminds us that there are limits to God's grace. One could make the case that Lot stayed in Sodom and became a civic leader because he thought he could make a godly difference (Gen 19:1 and 9 "acting like a judge"). After being warned, Lot lingered—trying to save his sons-in-law, but he could not. Even Abraham could not save the evil cities. When the appointed Day of the Lord comes, whether ultimately or in some partial measure, the door of grace closes (Matt 25:1–13, 2 Cor 5:9–11, 2 Pet 3:1–13). God's kindness in warning us of the deadliness of sin, the brevity of life, and the certainty of judgment stands as a huge act of grace.

Discussion

1. Is it fair to Scripture to describe Lot's story as a story of grace? Has this lesson made the case?
2. Even though grace triumphed, why is it important to remember that Lot bore terrible consequences for his sins?
3. Why would God choose to describe Lot as righteous and godly in 2 Peter 2? Why share this information with us?
4. Why might some over-apply Lot's story to the subject of grace?
5. Why might some be tempted to discount Peter's teachings about the righteousness of Lot?

2. JOSEPH AND HIS BROTHERS
ROBIN DUNAWAY

GENESIS 50:20

One Main Thing

Grace entails forgiveness, and the story of Joseph shows us a human example of forgiveness despite terrible sin.

Introduction

The story of Joseph is a vision of grace. The beginning of the story in Genesis 37 establishes the main characters: Joseph, his brothers, and their father, Jacob/Israel. This chapter also establishes the tension in the story, as the father obviously favors one child over the others, and makes sure everyone knows it (vv. 3–4), so that the other brothers grow resentful of the younger Joseph. Not only that, but Joseph has a couple of dreams (vv. 5–

11), which he—perhaps unwisely—tells to his brothers and father. The clear interpretation of these dreams is that Joseph will rule over the other members of his family, and whether the brothers think that Joseph is simply being arrogant or whether they secretly fear that his dreams will come true (after all, their father is clearly preparing Joseph for an exalted role), "they hated him even more because of his dream" (v. 8).

Going Deeper

Joseph's brothers play an important part in this vision of grace. They become the antagonists of the whole story, even until the end. They tend to be disobedient to their father, which would probably strain the relationship. As the relationship unfolds in the story, they become, in a negative way, the reason that their entire race is saved.

Joseph, Israel's favorite son, receives the special coat from his father (Gen 37:3). Part of the reason Jacob favors Joseph is because Joseph is obedient. The other sons are disobedient, as the demonstrated by the negative report that Joseph brings their father about his brothers (v. 2). There is an obvious ill effect in the brothers' relationship with Joseph for this reason. They are mortified that the father loves Joseph more than them, but seem to be unwilling to be obedient to the father, to make the relationship closer. Hence, the brothers hate Joseph because of his relationship with their father to him. So, when Joseph has the two dreams, this solidifies the hate that will soon become very evident by the following stories.

To understand this story, you must understand the concept of justice and mercy, because if you do not understand justice, you cannot remotely appreciate or fathom mercy. Justice is when you get what you deserve; it is the natural cause and effect ratio. Grace is the outward show of mercy. To have the proper vision of grace, one must also understand obedience to something other than himself. If there is no obedience, then justice rules. The created is subject to the Creator. If the Creator demands obedience, then justice is the outward show for disobedience. Forgiveness is what grace is all about, and without forgiveness there can never be reconciliation, only judgment. So, when we read the story of Joseph, we understand that Joseph's constant battle with forgiveness and his circumstance plays out for a larger purpose. It is no different with us, without forgiveness we can have no reconciliation either with our relationship with our Father in Heaven, or the people around us, even in our daily walk. While we look at the two greatest commands—love God and love each other—we see that will require much forgiveness from Him who is in heaven, or from each other as we tread on people daily.

The meat of Joseph's story begins when his father sends him to look for his brothers who are out tending the sheep (Gen 37:12–13). In his obedience, Joseph goes to look for the brothers, and cannot find them in the place that their father has sent them (v. 16).

This exacerbates the story problem, because in his obedience, he finds disobedience among his brothers. His brothers were told to go to Shechem, but they are actually found in Dothan (v. 17). When Joseph catches up with them, they know that they have been caught in their disobedience. This is when they decide to throw him down the well, and allow him to die there (vv. 19–20). Reuben, the only one with a conscience, tries to save him from the hands of his brothers (vv. 22, 29). He is somewhat successful, but is unable to prevent the brothers from selling Joseph to the Midianites (vv. 25–28).

In an effort to cover up what they had done, they scatter the blood of a lamb on Joseph's coat that was given to him as a gift by their father, they concoct a story that Joseph has been killed (vv. 31–35). Sin has a way of doing this, as it will create more sin, in the effort to cover up the first sin. But this very act sets up the scene, so that Joseph can eventually be in Egypt, in a position to be able to save the very ones who had set out to kill him. The irony here, is that the very act of Joseph's death creates life for the brothers.

The Midianites sell Joseph to Egypt. In Gen 39 Joseph has been delivered to Potiphar, where he is put in charge of Potiphar's household. Then Potiphar's wife sets Joseph up to have an affair with her. Because of Joseph's obedience to Potiphar, it causes her to accuse Joseph of something he did not do. This causes him to receive a prison sentence. But this misery allows Joseph to be in the right place at the right time, when he can interpret some dreams for a couple of people who know a very powerful person (Gen 40). And so, his faith is strong, and he endures, because God's hand is in his life. The dreams of Pharaoh's cupbearer and baker are interpreted by Joseph correctly. The baker lost his life, and the cupbearer was restored to his position. The only thing that Joseph asked for is that the cupbearer remember Joseph. Of course, he did not.

Now the big test is coming, because the Pharaoh himself has a couple dreams, that his wise men cannot interpret (Gen 41). The cupbearer finally remembers Joseph and how his own dreams were interpreted (vv. 9–13). The Pharaoh summons Joseph (v. 14). Joseph gives God the credit (v. 16). He tells the dream, as well as the meaning of the dream. And because of that he is put in charge of all of the Egyptian Kingdom (vv. 37–45). He has the express job to take the seven years of plenty and create storage so that they may prosper in the seven years of famine. This was the dream that Pharaoh had and that was interpreted and told by Joseph through God's power.

Application

Joseph always remembers that God is the one who has given him everything, including his ability. He understands that there's a larger picture to be seen. I believe this allows him to have the ability, not only to serve the pharaoh, but be able to forgive those who have trespassed against him along the way. This vision of grace seems to remain throughout Joseph's life. During the seven years of plenty, Joseph begins to plan, understanding that there will be seven years of famine. He diligently works to save the people. In the time of the famine, Joseph's father and brothers contemplate what to do for their own hunger (Gen 42:5). With starvation surely at hand, they hear that Egypt has grain. They decide to go to Egypt, where they have their first encounter, with Joseph. The emotions surely must have been strong for Joseph when he first saw the ones who actually left him for dead, and ultimately sold him into slavery to the Midianites. One could only imagine what that must have felt like. In his wisdom, he gives his brothers a chance to be saved. He asks about his father, and his younger brother Benjamin (42:13–16; 43:27–29; 45:3), who did not play a part in his demise. He uses his brothers to get to be with his father and his younger brother. The story unfolds, that he sends them back to their father with food, withholding one brother (42:24–26). This seems to be the down payment for him to get his family back to Egypt. All the while, Joseph must have a larger picture in place, as he strives to bring his family back together. At this point, his vision of grace must be at its strongest. His heavenly designation, coupled with his ability to forgive, is the grace that is needed to save Israel. When he finally reveals himself to his brothers, they are worried that he will take revenge on their actions against him. But in his vision of grace, "What you meant for evil, God meant for Good" (45:7; 50:20).

Conclusion

Joseph showed grace to his brothers, who had treated him terribly. His story serves as an example of God's grace and mercy toward us sinners, and as an example of the type of grace we should show toward others.

Discussion

1. Do you think Joseph's brothers felt guilty about what they had done to their brother?
2. How do you think Joseph felt when he first saw his brothers again, when they came to buy grain?
3. Do you think Joseph was ready to forgive his brothers immediately?
4. What parallels do you see between the story of Joseph and the story of Christ?

3. GRACE IN THE EXODUS

C. WAYNE KILPATRICK

EXODUS 34:6

One Main Thing

It is not man's favor to man, but rather God's grace and favor toward man that is our polar star. God is the origin of grace and favor, and we must strive to imitate him. God is our example in grace and favor and not man.

Introduction

Grace is used so many times in the Bible that it is almost overwhelming. The Old Testament contains more than 120 references to "grace" or variations of the word.[1] There is a close blending of Hebrew words meaning grace, mercy, favor, gracious, and sometimes the word "goodness."

We understand that grace is often defined as "underserved favor." There is also a sense of pity, compassion, and mercy contained in grace. When people show grace, they also show mercy. They show kindness and they demonstrate love.

In this study of Exodus 33:12–19, the focus is on the use of grace and favor. As we study this passage, we see it uses several terms for grace. Here the words "mercy" and goodness are used as well as the term "grace." The passage reads as follows:

> And Moses said unto the LORD, See, thou sayest unto me, bring up this people: and thou hast not let me know whom thou wilt send with me. Yet thou hast said, I know thee by name, and thou hast also found **grace** in my sight. Now therefore, I pray thee, if I have found **grace** in thy sight, shew me now thy way, that I may know thee, that I may find grace in thy sight: and consider that this nation is thy people. And he said, My presence shall go with thee, and I will give thee rest. And he said unto him, if thy presence goes not with me, carry us not up hence. For wherein shall it be known here that I and thy people have found **grace** in thy sight? is it not in that thou goest with us? so shall we be separated, I and thy people, from all the people that are upon the face of the earth. And the LORD said unto Moses, I will do this thing also that thou hast spoken: for thou hast found **grace** in my sight, and I know thee

by name. And he said, I beseech thee, shew me thy glory. And he said, I will make all my **goodness** pass before thee, and I will proclaim the name of the LORD before thee; and will be **gracious** to whom I will be **gracious** and will shew **mercy** on whom I will shew **mercy**.[2]

Every appearance of "grace" or "gracious" in these verses comes from the Hebrew word *ḥēn*,[3] while the word "mercy" comes from *raḥam* and "goodness" in v. 19 is from *tuv*. All of these qualities of God are summed up in God's self-revelation quoted at the beginning of this chapter (Exod 34:6), which uses the same word "gracious,"[4] as well as "merciful" (*raḥum*), and the important word ḥesed, translated there "goodness."

Going Deeper

In Exodus 33:12–19 Moses found favor in God's sight. We do not know how this favor was found. We would normally think that Moses did something good to find this favor. Indeed, he had already done many good things by taking God's people from Egypt. But before the exodus, Moses had done more things wrong than right. The biggest thing was the murdering of an Egyptian and his attempt to cover the act up by running away, revealing his guilt. For forty years he lived in the desert—a seeming failure. However, he approached the burning bush and discovered Jehovah.

If we think that Moses had deserved any of this special treatment, then we are mistaken. Here we begin to see where the meaning of the word "favor" leads us.

In this text the use of the word 'favor' (*ḥēn*) signals that Moses is inferior to God. We understand that a man is dependent upon God. Moses was greatly in need of God's favor, and God had the power to help. He decided to give this grace to Moses as a favor, though he was not obligated to do so. The beauty of God's grace is that it is an attribute of him who changes not —taught throughout the Old and New Testament.

The only thing that changed about God is the way in which he revealed his grace. God is equally as gracious in the Old Testament as he is in the New Testament. However, one must focus harder to see God's grace in the Old Testament. In the New Testament grace is more easily recognized because Jesus is the focal point of God's grace. The Bible is very clear about the unchanging nature of God. James declares that every good gift "cometh down from the Father of lights, with whom is no variableness, neither shadow of turning." Hebrews 13:8 tells us that Jesus Christ is "the same yesterday, and today, and forever." If that is true, it follows that there has not been a change, nor could ever be, any change in God's character.

In Exodus 4:27–31, God demonstrated grace. The children of Israel had done nothing to warrant favor from God, yet God initiated contact with them in response to their cries about their bondage. God reached out to a group of people that was unable to reach out to him. God selected Moses and Aaron to be his mouth-piece so that the children of Israel could focus on God's work and to witness the favor he was about to show. God proved he was willing and able to liberate the children of Israel from their bondage before the people provided any merits proving worthiness. This is echoed in the New Testament passage of Romans 5:8, as the Apostle wrote: "But God commendeth his love toward us, in that, while we were yet sinners, Christ died for us." This theme is throughout the old Testament and shows that God revealed his grace and favor through action, even when the people did not deserve it. All the grace and favor shown by God has do with salvation. Remember Moses' words as Israel was about to cross the Red Sea:

> And Moses said unto the people, Fear ye not, stand still, and see the salvation of the Lord, which he will show to you today: for the Egyptians whom ye have seen today, ye shall see them again no more forever. (Exod 14:13)

Exodus was written to celebrate God's gracious deliverance of Israel from the Egyptian slavery. This brought them into a covenant relationship with him. Throughout the book of Exodus, the celebration of grace and kindness is shown toward them in this deliverance—this salvation.

Application

In a similar way the book of Exodus leads New Testament Christians to celebrate God's grace and his glorious deliverance of his spiritual Israel from the slavery of sin into a covenant relationship and fellowship with him and his dear son Jesus Christ. Since God is the same in the Old Testament as in the New Testament, and there is "no variableness, neither shadow of turning" (Jas 1:17), we can count on God's grace being the same toward us as it was toward ancient Israel. The way God reveals his grace is the only thing that has changed about him. It is still the same grace as it has always been and still does the same job it has always done. It is still unearned grace and favor from God as with Israel, so it is today for Christians. As God gave grace to Israel while they were in a sinful state, his response toward us was "while we were yet sinners, Christ died for us" (Rom 5:8). There is still an action we must perform to receive this gift given of God—not to earn it, but to receive it. We must either accept it or reject it; that is the action we must perform to receive this gift from God.

In the English New Testament, the word "grace" is always a translation of *charis*, a word that occurs in the Greek text more than 170 times. Grace is often discussed in relation to salvation:

> This righteousness is given through faith in Jesus Christ to all who believe. There is no difference between Jew and Gentile, for all have sinned and come short of the glory of God, and all are justified freely by his grace through the redemption that came by Christ Jesus. (Rom 3:22–24)

A question arises from this text. What does "to all who believe" mean? Biblically a believer is one who not only gives mental assent, but one who responds with an action after giving mental assent. See the examples of this in Hebrews 11. Sixteen times the phrase "by faith" or "through faith" was immediately followed by an action on the part of the person who acted upon his or her faith. After the action was performed, God gave his favor. Think of this in this way—if a person falls overboard from a seagoing vessel and someone throws him or her a lifeline, the person is not saved until pulled to safety. The one who threw the lifeline was not obligated to throw the line, but by grace he or she threw it. Now the person who was pulled to safety had to do something even though the line was given through the grace of the person who threw it. The one in the water had to decide to take hold of the line and continue holding on until he or she was safe. That is the way God's grace works. He has extended it to all, but only those who decide to do what it takes to receive it will enjoy the grace that is freely given of God. "For the grace of God that bringeth salvation, hath appeared to all men" (Titus 2:11). The grace is there, and it can be freely received or rejected. The choice ours.

Conclusion

Christians gain confidence in the grace of God upon studying Exodus, because of the repeated use of grace towards Moses and Israel. Neither Moses nor Israel had earned God's grace, yet God showered his grace upon them, even while they were in a sinful state. Since God never changes, he will respond accordingly toward us today.

> And for this cause, he is the mediator of the new testament, that by means of death, for the redemption of the transgressions that were under the first testament, they which are called might receive the promise of eternal inheritance. (Heb 9:15)

> For the promise is unto you, and to your children, and to all that are afar off, even as many as the Lord our God shall call. (Acts 2:39)

Israel was called by the word of God through the prophets, and we are called by the word of God, as recorded on the written pages which are given by inspiration of God. We will receive God's grace and favor if we keep a penitent heart and continue to trust in him and his holy word.

Discussion

1. Does God owe us his grace because of our righteousness?
2. How are grace, mercy, favor, and kindness equal in the Bible?
3. How was grace in the book of Exodus connected to salvation?
4. Is grace connected to salvation in the New Testament?

Endnotes

1. On the various Hebrew and Greek words translated "grace," see this volume's Introduction.

2. All scripture references are from the KJV, unless otherwise specified.

3. The "gracious" statements in v. 19 are actually from the related verb *ḥanan*.

4. It is actually the adjectival form, *ḥannun*.

4. GRACE IN THE BOOK OF RUTH

NATHAN DAILY

Ruth 1:16–17

One Main Thing

The story of Naomi's reversal from emptiness to fullness in the book of Ruth offers readers an opportunity to consider how divine guidance and human initiative may work in tandem to provide renewal and hope, through the grace of God, to those in need.

Introduction

The book of Ruth is a short story of a family's care, kindness, and fidelity toward one another in the midst of overwhelming circumstances. The story appears in four scenes. After introducing the problem in the first scene, a different character enacts a plan in three subsequent scenes. The book of Ruth is structured as follows:

I. Famine, Death, and Return (1:1–22)

II. Ruth's Plan: Ruth Gleans in Boaz's Field (2:1–23)

III. Naomi's Plan: Ruth Meets Boaz at the Threshing Floor (3:1–18)

IV. Boaz's Plan: Boaz Marries Ruth (4:1–22)

The book tells of a woman from Judah, Naomi, who returns to Bethlehem from Moab after experiencing the death of her husband and two sons. After Naomi's daughter-in-law, Ruth, refuses to leave her side, the two widows begin a struggle for survival by searching for food and, eventually, concocting a dangerous plan whereby Ruth proposes marriage to Boaz, a relative of Naomi's late husband. Once Boaz determines that a closer relative is not willing to marry Ruth, Boaz and Ruth are married and give birth to a son who ultimately becomes the grandfather of David. The entirety of the story presents the gracious actions of individuals as reflections of key attributes of God known from God's past actions on behalf of Israel.

Going Deeper

Investigation into the portrayal of grace in the book of Ruth can begin by considering one of the book's prominent themes: emptiness to fullness.[1]

The beginning of the story presents Naomi's life as becoming increasingly characterized by emptiness.

Naomi and her family are forced to leave their home because, ironically, there is a famine in Bethlehem (lit. "house of bread"). In spite of the family's attempt to escape starvation, Naomi's life spirals into crisis as her husband and two sons die in Moab. The narrator's language highlights the increasing emptiness in Naomi's life with each experience of death: "she was left with her two sons" (1:3), "the woman was left without her two sons and without her husband" (1:5). In the span of a few short verses, Naomi looses her status as wife and mother, now only known as the woman (1:5), and is left alone with two daughters-in-law in a world where the security of a woman primarily lies with a husband and male descendants.[2] After experiencing loss on multiple levels and now in a position without hope (1:12), Naomi returns to her homeland and explicitly states her situation in terms of emptiness and fullness:

> "Do not call me Naomi [lit. "pleasant"]," she replied. "Call me Mara [lit. "bitter"]," for Shaddai has made my lot very bitter. I went away full, and YHWH has brought me back empty. How can you call me Naomi, when YHWH has dealt harshly with me, when Shaddai has brought misfortune upon me! (Ruth 1:20–21)

Even though Naomi was, in fact, in threat of starving from famine in Bethlehem, she depicts this time of her life as full and pleasant in comparison to the empty and bitter life she now faces without her husband and sons.

After the stark depiction of Naomi's loss, the action in three subsequent scenes[3] presents Naomi's steady reversal from emptiness to fullness. By repeatedly using a single Hebrew root word (g'l, often translated "redeem" or "kinsman"),[4] the author stresses the concept of "redemption" as being crucial for reaching the resolution to Naomi's crisis. In the Hebrew Bible, a redeemer is a close relative who takes responsibility for various acts including the repurchase of property.[5] When a family member is forced to sell land because of financial difficulty, the redeemer can purchase the land so that it will remain with the family. More generally, a redeemer is one who delivers another from any type of danger.[6] In the Book of Ruth, this root refers to both the person who redeems as well as the act of redemption. It is Naomi's recognition of Boaz as a redeemer from whom she can expect assistance[7] for herself and Ruth that provides Naomi's first acknowledgment of hope that her situation can change (2:20). Beyond food Naomi does not appear to know the extent of what this redeemer will provide; however, by the end of the story Boaz wants to redeem the land of Elimelech and, in addition, marry Ruth (4:4–5, 10). Ultimately, Naomi's life exhibits an unexpected fullness achieved through a child born to Ruth and Boaz. The child is characterized as a "redeemer" who will renew Naomi's life and sustain her in her old age (4:14–15). The word translated "renew" or "return" (4:15) most clearly highlights Naomi's reversal from emptiness to fullness.[8] Previously, upon her return to Bethlehem, Naomi used this word at the depth of her despair exclaiming: "YHWH returned me empty" (1:21). With the birth of Ruth's child as her redeemer, Naomi is no longer empty but has been returned to life.

Application

Attention to the theme of emptiness to fullness in the book of Ruth provides an opportunity to consider how acts of favor or grace are central to Naomi's unexpected reversal. Two examples suggest how God's people might reflect upon the portrayal of grace in the ancient story of Naomi in order to enact God's grace in contemporary contexts in hope that the lives of ourselves and others can move from emptiness to fullness.

1. Grace, manifest through fidelity and redemption and born out of a trust in God's ability to act, appears in the book of Ruth within an interplay between divine guidance and human initiative. The book does not contain miracles or direct speech from God and primarily focuses on the interaction between members of a single family; however, the book is not devoid of theology. Two direct statement of God's activity bracket the beginning and ending of the story. God brings an end to the famine (1:6) and, thereby, provides initial

possibility for movement toward Naomi's redemption. Also, God allows Ruth to conceive and bear a child (4:13). Therefore, the two factors that led to Naomi's emptiness (famine and childlessness) are overcome by the only two actions of God.[9]

The interaction between human characters, rather than the action of God, dominates the story. Central to understanding the nature of the grace exhibited by the characters are their numerous displays of *hesed*.[10] This Hebrew word is translated as "fidelity," "kindness," "loyalty," "loving kindness," or "steadfast love" and is often characterized by a care that exceeds expectations by taking "action to rescue [another] from a situation of desperate need."[11] Throughout the story the main characters express fidelity toward one another. Naomi concocts a dangerous plan for the sole purpose of finding a home for Ruth (3:1–5). Ruth is recognized for the *hesed* she shows as she leaves all she knows to follow Naomi to a foreign country (1:8, 16–17), as she works hard gleaning to provide for Naomi (2:7, 17), and as she chooses to marry Boaz in order to provide help to Naomi rather than choosing a husband for her own interests (3:10).[12] Before he knows he is a redeemer for Naomi, Boaz shows concern and makes special allowances for Ruth as she gleans in his field (2:8–20). After realizing his role as a redeemer, Boaz goes beyond what others are willing to do in order to care for Ruth and Naomi as well as provide for the name of Elimelech (4:1–10).

Even when God is not present in the narrative as the characters strategize to maneuver themselves toward a more hopeful future, the repeated references to God in the book's dialogue indicate they trust God is capable of acting on their behalf.[13] Often taking the form of prayer,[14] this dialogue commends the kindness or actions of another and states a belief that God will provide blessing. These prayers are ultimately fulfilled during the story. A striking example is Boaz's prayer for Ruth as she gleans in the field: "May YHWH reward your deeds. May you have a full recompense from YHWH, the God of Israel, under whose wings you have sought refuge" (2:12). The prayer is surprisingly fulfilled when Ruth unexpectedly proposes marriage to Boaz[15] at the threshing floor: "I am your handmaid Ruth. Spread your robe [lit. wing] over your handmaid, for you are a redeeming kinsman." The prayer is fulfilled as Boaz takes action and agrees to Ruth's request. Whereas God will provide for Ruth (4:13), the wordplay highlights that this will only happen when Boaz, who offered the prayer, spreads his "wing" and marries Ruth, thereby, providing the impetus for the fulfillment of his own prayer.[16]

Readers are presented with a fascinating interaction between human initiative and divine guidance that occurs as humans must act to change their plight from emptiness to fullness, while at the same time acknowledging their trust that God will provide blessing. God's two sole actions (1:6; 4:13) underscore the fact that only God can solve the crisis of the story.[17] At the same time, the characters' dialogue reflects an expectation that God will reward human *hesed* ("fidelity") by showing divine *hesed*.[18] The emphasis on human initiative confronts and causes the reader to consider emulation of these characters that live a life characterized by fidelity and kindness.[19] This fidelity is epitomized in Ruth's famous words that not only state her unending loyalty but also provide a pattern for readers who are considering the theological implications of the text: "Do not urge me to leave you, to turn back and not follow you. For wherever you go, I will go; wherever you lodge, I will lodge; your people shall be my people, and your God my God" (1:16–17).

2. When the book of Ruth is read in concert with the story of God, the grace performed by the characters in the story appears as an exhibition of God's attributes, known from and previously experienced through God's own actions. In the Christian Bible, the book of Ruth follows the story of the increasingly downward spiral of leadership within Israel in the book of Judges, which culminates with rape, war, and anarchy (Judg 19–21). Ruth presents an ordinary family, living during the same time period, that acts out of kindness and interest toward others and, thereby, provides a sharp contrast to the self-interest that typifies the end of the book of Judges (Judg 21:25). As Judges ends with the claim that only a king can remedy the situation, Ruth offers a story of the origin

of the Davidic monarchy that will be the focus of the narration in the book of Samuel. The placement of Ruth between these two books encourages readers to approach Ruth within the context of a broad storyline of God's interaction with and actions on behalf of the people of Israel.

As mentioned earlier, God acts only twice in the book of Ruth (1:6; 4:13); however, when placed in the broader storyline of Israel and her God, the reader will notice the two key terms "redeemer/redemption" and "fidelity" (*hesed*) are often words used to describe the character and actions of the God of Israel. The term *ḥesed* is used throughout the Hebrew Bible as a defining feature of God's character.[20] God shows *hesed* to many[21] and will do so forever.[22] As a redeemer, God delivers those who are weak or in need from trouble.[23] God's role as redeemer is emphasized at key points within the story of Israel as God redeems Israel from Egypt[24] and exile,[25] thereby, providing hope for future redemption.[26] Since these actions describe humans rather than God in Ruth, when the book placed within the story of God's action toward Israel, the reader sees that the redemption and fidelity that often characterize the deity, at times, also must be demonstrated by humans who work to exude the attributes and actions of God in their own lives so that kindness and redemption may be available to those in need.

Conclusion

The book of Ruth is a short story of the kindness, fidelity, and trust of a family living in the midst of chaos; yet, the book is also a challenge to consider the impact a family may have if it knows the story of God, trusts in that God, and chooses God's own attributes as models for emulation. Through this choice to practice fidelity and offer redemption in order to reflect God's grace toward those in need, the people of God are able to more clearly live their hope, the hope to experience fidelity and redemption from their God.

Discussion

1. Describe the theme of emptiness to fullness in the book of Ruth.
2. Who is the main character in the book of Ruth? Who are the other characters? Describe the actions and motivations of each character in the book.
3. As the characters in the book of Ruth speak, they consistently state various attributes of God and express expectation that God will act. How do you imagine they are able to speak this way? What might help us speak this way? How do we develop trust in God's

promises like the characters of the book of
Ruth?

4. How do divine guidance and human activity
   work together as the conflict in the book of
   Ruth is resolved?

5. How does the book of Ruth help us
   understand the concepts of fidelity and
   redemption? How might we express fidelity
   and redemption in our context?

6. How does the book of Ruth help us
   understand and tell the story of God? What
   does this short book have to say about who
   God is and what God is doing in the world?

7. The book of Ruth portrays the care and love
   of a family during the very normal turns of
   life. How do these simple actions impact the
   immediate and the future? How might
   exhibiting kindness in the mundane
   moments of life have a lasting impact? Can
   you think of any examples?

8. How can we as the people of God both
   individually and collectively exhibit
   characteristics of God in our community?
   What characteristics do we exhibit now?
   What characteristics do we need to
   work on?

Endnotes

1. See D. F. Rauber, "Literary Values in the Bible: The Book of Ruth," *Journal of Biblical Literature* 89 (1970): 27–37. On the interpretation of Ruth see, Frederic W. Bush, *Ruth, Esther*, WBC 9 (Dallas: Word, 1996); Kirsten Nielsen, *Ruth*, OTL (Louisville: Westminster, 1997); Eugene H. Peterson, *Five Smooth Stones for Pastoral Work* (Grand Rapids: Eerdmans, 1980); K. Lawson Younger, *Judges/Ruth*, NIVAC (Grand Rapids: Zondervan, 2002); Katharine Doob Sakenfeld, *Ruth*, Int (Louisville: John Knox, 1999).

2. Adele Berlin, *Poetics and Interpretation of Biblical Narrative* (Sheffield: Almond, 1883), 87.3. Ruth 2:1–23; 3:1–18; 4:1–17.

4. The root g'l is found 23 times in the book of Ruth. See, 2:20; 3:9, 12 (2x), 13 (4x); 4:1, 3, 4 (5x), 6 (5x), 7, 8, 14.

5. Lev 25:25–34, 47–55; Num 35:9–28; Jer 32:6–15.

6. Bush, 137. See, Gen 48:16; Ps 72:14; 107:2; Lam 3:53–58.

7. Nielsen, 63–64.

8. Sakenfeld, 82. "Return" (Heb. šwv) is a keyword throughout the book (1:6, 7, 8, 10, 11, 12, 15, 16, 21, 22; 2:6; 4:3, 15).

9. Nielsen, 30.

10. Ruth 1:8; 2:20; 3:10.

11. Sakenfeld, 11–12.

12. Nielsen, 76.

13. The dialogue of the characters mentions God at 1:8, 9, 13, 16, 17, 20, 21; 2:4, 12, 20; 3:10, 13; 4:11, 12, 14.

14. Cf. Ruth 1:8; 2:12, 20; 3:10.

15. Cf. Ezek 16:8.

16. Bush, 55; Rauber, 32.

17. W. S. Prinsloo, "The Theology of the Book of Ruth," *Vetus Testamentum* 30 (1980): 330–341.

18. Ruth 1:8; 3:10; cf. 2:12. See, Nielsen, 31.

19. Bush, 42–47, 52–55

20. Exod 34:6–7; Num 14:18; Neh 9:17; Ps 86:15; Joel 2:13; Jonah 4:2.

21. Exod 20:6; Deut 5:10; 7:9.

22. 1 Chron 16:34; 2 Chron 7:3; Ezra 3:11; Ps 100:5; 106:1; Jer 33:11.

23. Prov 23:10–11; Job 19:25; Jer 50:34; Ps 106:10; Hos 13:14; Ps 107:2–3.

24. Exod 6:6; 15:13.

25. Isa 44:22; 48:17; Jer 31:11; Mic 4:10

26. Isa 59:20; 60:16.

5. THE CHALLENGE OF LOVE
ED GALLAGHER

HOSEA 1–2; 11

One Main Thing

The marriage between Hosea and Gomer presents to us a picture of our gracious, loving God, and calls on us to imitate God by loving others even when it hurts.

Introduction

Hosea lived in the eighth century BC, according to the first verse of the book. The kings named there all reigned between about 750–700 BC. That dating makes Hosea more-or-less a contemporary of a few other prophets: Amos, Micah, and Isaiah name some of the same kings in the first verses of their books, and Jonah also lived at this same time (cf. 2 Kings 14:25). But Hosea is unique among this group of prophets; in fact, he's unique among all prophets, because he's the only northern prophet for whom we have a book of oracles. Remember that after the death of Solomon, the kingdom of Israel split in two (cf. 1 Kings 12), into a northern kingdom called Israel and a southern kingdom called Judah. Almost all the prophets who have books named after them are from the south, the nation of Judah. That's true of Isaiah, Amos, Micah, and most of the others. Jonah is from the north (again, see 2 Kings 14:25), but we don't have a book of Jonah's oracles, we just have a story about Jonah (with one, very brief oracle; Jonah 3:4). Amos, like Hosea, did prophesy to the northern nation of Israel, but Amos was actually from the south (see Amos 1:1; 7:12–15). So the book of Hosea—alone among all the books of the Bible—preserves for us a collection of oracles form a northern prophet.

As soon as Jeroboam the son of Nebat founded the northern nation of Israel, he established a state-sponsored religion centered around veneration of golden cows, one in Dan in the far north, another in Bethel close to the border with Judah (1 Kings 12:26–33). As in the case of the golden cow that Aaron made for the people at Sinai (Exod 32:1–6), these cows in Dan and Bethel were probably supposed to be idols of Yahweh, Israel's God. Jeroboam identifies the cow as representing the one "who brought you up from the land of Egypt" (1 Kings 12:28; cf. Exod 32:4). This sin of worshiping Yahweh through an idol defiled the northern nation of Israel throughout their history. At their best, the northerners were idolaters.

When Ahab came to the throne of Israel, things got worse. "Then, as if following the sin of Jeroboam son of Nebat were not enough, he married Jezebel, the daughter of Ethbaal king of the Sidonians, and then proceeded to serve Baal and bow in worship to him" (1 Kings 16:31). No longer were they idolaters; now they were pagans, worshiping foreign gods. You remember Elijah's contest on Mt. Carmel with the prophets of Baal (1 Kings 18), and the Lord's words that there were 7000 (only!) who had not bowed the knee to Baal (19:18).

A century later, in the days of a second Jeroboam —this one, the son of Jehoash (cf. 2 Kings 14:23–29)— the situation was largely the same, as we see in Hosea.

Going Deeper

God called Hosea to do something pretty strange, something that we would never advise our own children to do. God told Hosea to go find himself an unfaithful woman and marry her (1:2). Of course, when God gives these strange commands—such as telling Isaiah to walk around naked (Isa 20) or telling Ezekiel to lie on his side for more than a year (Ezek 4)—he does so in order to prove a point. Hosea's marriage with Gomer, the unfaithful woman, will provide a living demonstration of what God's relationship with Israel is like.

Israel is the unfaithful woman.

> Yes, their mother is promiscuous; she conceived them and acted shamefully. For she thought, "I will follow my lovers, the men who give me my food and water, my wool and flax, my oil and drink." (2:5)
>
> She does not recognize that it is I who gave her the grain, the new wine, and the fresh oil. I lavished silver and good on her, which they used for Baal. (2:8)

The entire book of Hosea is a meditation on the unfaithfulness of Israel. Chapter 4 details sin after sin. The problem is, of course, that they worship Baal, but also that they worship that cow in Bethel (which Hosea derisively calls Beth-aven, "house of sin," rather than Bethel, "house of God"; 4:15). The problem is the priests, who do not teach (4:4), the prophets, who prophesy lies (4:5). "My people are destroyed for lack of knowledge" (4:6).

> My people consult their wooden idols, and their divining rods inform them. For a spirit of promiscuity leads them astray; they act promiscuously in disobedience to their God. (4:12)

But the book of Hosea, even more so, is a meditation on the love of God. Hosea the prophet is an image of God. What God wants to communicate through this marriage of the prophet and the harlot is not only how unfaithful Israel has been, but how much pain Israel's unfaithfulness has caused God—pain out of God's deep love for his people.

Hear God, the wounded lover, speak about his dear one.

She does not recognize
that it is I who gave her the grain,
the new wine, and the fresh oil.
I lavished silver and gold on her,
which they used for Baal. (2:8)
Therefore, I am going to persuade her,
lead her to the wilderness and speak tenderly to her.
(2:14)

God wants to take Israel back to the beginning of their relationship, where they went on their first date, in a manner of speaking. God is angry and hurt, but even more so he longs for the relationship to be restored. He just wants his people back. So he will court his wife again. Once he gets Israel back to the wilderness, God has it all planned out.

There I will give her vineyards back to her and make the Valley of Achor into a gateway of hope.

There she will respond as she did in the days of her youth, as in the day she came out of the land of Egypt. In that day, says the Lord, you will call me "My husband" and no longer "My baal." For I will remove the names of the Baals from her mouth; they will no longer be remembered by their names. (2:15–17)

Even though baal is sometimes just a Hebrew word meaning "husband," God said he didn't want Israel using that word anymore, because it sounds too much like Israel's ex-boyfriend. What God wants more than anything is not to punish Israel but to love Israel and be loved in return.

The image of a marriage is not the only image Hosea uses to depict God's relationship with Israel. Another way of looking at it is that God is Israel's father, and Israel is the disobedient son.

> When Israel was a child I loved him,
> > and out of Egypt I called my son. (11:1)

God is the tender-hearted father who lavishes gifts on his child.

> It was I who taught Ephraim to walk,
> > taking them by the hand,
> > but they never knew that I healed them.
> > I led them with human cords,

with ropes of love.

To them I was like one who eases the yoke from
their jaws;

I bent down to give them food. (11:3–4)

But Israel is so disobedient, God decides to punish
his son (11:2, 6–7). Then the unexpected happens—God
has a change of heart. He cannot give up on his
beloved son, which leads to "an utterance whose
daring is unparalleled in the whole of prophecy."[1]

How can I give you up, Ephraim?
How can I surrender you, Israel?
How can I make you like Admah?
How can I treat you like Zeboiim?
I have had a change of heart;
my compassion is stirred!
I will not vent the full fury of my anger;
I will not turn back to destroy Ephraim.
For I am God and not man,
the Holy One among you;
I will not come in rage. (11:8–9)

God is like the father in the Parable of the Prodigal
Son. (In fact, God is the father in the Parable of the
Prodigal Son.) The younger son abandons his family
and burns through his inheritance doing all the things
his father had warned him about. And when this
prodigal son decides to return home, there is his father,

standing at the edge of their property, peering into the horizon on the lookout for his boy (Luke 15:20). Sure, there had no doubt been moments when this father had been angry with his son, had thought to himself, "If I ever see that boy again, why I'll ...." But when it came right down to it, the father just wanted a relationship with his son. When the boy came back, the father felt no bitterness, just delight.

Application

God calls on Hosea to be an image of God. God calls on his servants to be an image of God. And in the case of the book of Hosea, God is the wounded lover, the hurting father, longing for relationship with his people. He calls on us to do the same. God calls on his people to love at the risk of a broken heart.

In the movie Room (2015), a mom has to convince her small son to help her escape from their abductor, so she tells him a story, explaining things he doesn't understand. At one point, this boy looks up at his mom and yells, "I want a different story!" and the mom yells back, "No! This is the story that you get!"[2]

There are many times that we'd like a different story. Right after Peter had confessed Jesus as the Messiah, and then Jesus started to explain about his impending death—teaching for which Peter was not at all ready—Peter essentially looked at Jesus and said, "I want a different story" (cf. Mark 8:27–33). But Jesus had to tell Peter, "No, this is the story that you get." I bet Paul sometimes wished he didn't have to endure all these hardships in order to bring salvation to the world (2 Cor 11:24–29). But that is the story that God had prepared for Paul (Acts 9:16).

I can imagine Hosea looking up to heaven and saying, "I want a different story. I don't want to marry this unfaithful woman. I don't want to go find her again. It hurts too much." And God responds, "No, Hosea, this is the story that you get. You have been called to image me. And that means you must love even when it hurts, because that's who I am."

Followers of Christ love others even when it hurts. There are times in our families that it gets hard to love people, but we will love them even when it hurts. It gets hard in church sometimes to love fellow Christians, but if we are going to imitate God, we will love people even when it hurts.

When my wife and I first decided to get involved in foster care, one older member of our church who had fostered children decades earlier told me, "Prepare to have your heart broken." He meant that foster parents take in kids who have been in some pretty rough situations, and the foster kids become a part of this new family. Foster parents provide for these kids, and support them, attend their school functions and their sporting events; foster parents love their foster kids.

And then, usually, after a while, a state agent comes and removes the children from the foster home and

puts them back in a situation that is—shall we say?—
less than ideal. And it breaks your heart. So, what?
Should you not love these kids at all? That is no kind
of solution for people who imitate God, because our
God loves even when it hurts.

Conclusion

What is the message of Hosea? Paul sums it up well.

So be imitators of God, as beloved children, and
live in love, as Christ loved us and handed himself over
for us as a sacrificial offering to God for a fragrant
aroma. (Eph 5:1–2)

Hosea is a vision of grace, because he is an image of
our God.

Discussion

1. Why do you think God told Hosea to marry
   an unfaithful woman? (Hos 1:2)
2. What do you think you would have done if
   you received the command from God that
   Hosea received?
3. Which image of God do you find more
   compelling: God as the broken-hearted
   husband (Hos 1–2), or God as the grieving
   father (Hos 11)?
4. What was a time in your life when you had

to make a conscious decision to love someone who was not very loveable?

5. What struggles do you think Hosea had in imitating God's love? What struggles do Christians today have?

Endnotes

1. Gerhard von Rad, *Old Testament Theology*, 2 vols. (New York: Harper & Row, 1965), 2.145.

2. You can see the scene on YouTube; search "Room I want a different story."

 A BIG FISH STORY

TRAVIS HARMON

The Book of Jonah

One Main Thing

Stories of grace do not always appear as a "Vision of Grace" when you are living in the story. In fact, most of the time, grace sneaks up when you aren't expecting it.

Introduction

Jonah is a fascinating book. It is like no other book in the entire Bible. Usually, we think of it as a kids' story, but Jonah is not just a Bible story for children. It is funny how certain things get relegated to being for kids. We think of "Jesus Loves Me" as being just for kids. How do we get stuck in those ruts of thought? Jesus really does love us, and the Bible really does tell us so. We probably should spend more time thinking about just how much he really does love us and how the Bible really does tell us so rather than just dismissing it as for children.

Likewise, the book of Jonah has often been thought of as just a kids' story so we rarely study it in-depth. Usually we only look at Jonah 1–3 because those chapters fit in the kids' story concept, and we disregard chapter 4 because it is just way too deep for most kids and probably for a lot of adults.

In Chapter 1, the word of the Lord comes to Jonah and tells him to go to Nineveh. Nineveh was an ancient city located in Assyria (modern-day Iraq), and it is commonly thought that, at one time, it was the largest city in the world. Assyria was a longtime enemy of Israel, earning it several negative mentions in the Old Testament. A prophet Jonah, son of Amittai, is also mentioned in 2 Kings 14:25, which tells us the time period Jonah lived (mid-eighth century BC) and that he was a northerner, from the Israelite town of Gath-hepher. (Assyria destroyed Jonah's country, and maybe his hometown, in 722 BC.) The passage in 2 Kings also shows us that God, ironically, uses an evil king and Jonah to help to save some Israelites that had been subjugated and were being bitterly oppressed.

Going Deeper

In Chapter 1, Jonah runs from God's command. He is told to go, yet he flees in the opposite direction to the end of the known world. Jonah boards a ship to Tarshish, and God sends a storm to bring him back. The sailors do everything they can to save Jonah, but eventually are reluctantly convinced to throw him overboard at his own urging. When the storm immediately ceases, the sailors know it was an act of God, and they start to worship and make vows to the Lord. At the very end of the chapter, Jonah is swallowed by a great fish that God has prepared to receive him.

In Chapter 2, Jonah's circumstances help him decide to have a little talk with God. I am sure everyone has had that experience, maybe not from the belly of a fish, but when we feel that everything is not going to be okay, we tend to start looking for him; so does Jonah. It is from the belly of the fish that Jonah prays, and God hears him. God saves him by having the fish spit him out on the land.

In Chapter 3, the word of the Lord again comes to Jonah and tells him to go to Nineveh. This time Jonah, possibly wiser, but no softer and no less stubborn, obeys. In 3:4, we have the entire recorded text of Jonah's sermon: "Yet forty days, and Nineveh shall be overthrown!" It's not a beautiful oration on the love of God calling them to repentance. Jonah is the worst preacher ever! His sermon is eight words long, and he wanted his listeners to not respond. Yet, everyone in Nineveh does. Some may try to use this as an argument for shorter sermons because his eight-word sermon actually worked! The King orders everyone to repent. The

King is hopeful that God will show them mercy, and he does; God does not destroy Nineveh.

This is where we typically end the story. We tell the story of Jonah, but we leave off the rest because it is odd and doesn't fit our neat outline of the book.

Jonah ran

- from God in chapter 1,
- to God in chapter 2, and
- with God in chapter 3.

The first three chapters of Jonah are so fanciful some people have trouble accepting them; but to me, the really odd part of Jonah comes in the last chapter. Jonah is furious that God does not destroy Nineveh. He is so furious, in fact, that he again prays to God. But this time, instead of asking for God to save him, he prays that God will kill him! Then Jonah tells us why he ran away in the first place. What would send a man scurrying away from the command of the almighty God? Jonah knew God is just too nice and loving, and he knew that God would relent from his anger if the people repented.

Jonah hopes that God will repent from his kindness and destroy the city anyway. He goes up on a hill to watch to see what will happen. God makes a vine that shades Jonah, and Jonah is really happy about his little shading plant. The next day, God has a worm kill the plant and then, like at the beginning, He sends a wind. This time it is a harsh, hot, east wind. Jonah is so angry that when God asks him about the plant, Jonah says he is mad enough to die over it. This is a powerful object lesson for us and for Jonah who is acting like a horrible child. God asks Jonah: "If you want to save a plant that you didn't make and only lasted a day, then why can't I want to save a city with 120,000 little children and numerous animals." Yes, God cares for the babies and even for the cattle of Nineveh. What an amazing comparison between the love of God and the lack of it from Jonah. Jonah, the man of God, is the villain in the story and yet, amazingly, God still loves him, too.

Application

Jonah is a book of opposites. Everyone in the story is a stereotype, and every stereotype does the exact opposite of what one might think they would. Jonah, the prophet, disobeys, rebels and hates. The pagan sailors aren't hardened pirate-like killers; they are kind and concerned about a stranger and about maintaining their own innocence. The Ninevite king isn't cruel and blasphemous; he is humble and repentant. One might expect that he would have tried to have Jonah killed or expelled from the city, yet he heeds Jonah's miserable message. The sea and the storm are not indiscriminate killers; the fish, the worm, and the vine are not just nature-taking-its-course but are instead obedient servants of God. And perhaps most surprisingly to us, but not to Jonah, God is not the vengeance-hungry being that we expect. He is kind and merciful, overly so, to Jonah's way of thinking.

We truncate the last chapter of Jonah's story, but when we do, we are truncating the best part of God and Jonah's story. We are cutting off a display of amazing grace! The grace that saved the sailors, that saved Jonah, and that saved all of Nineveh! God cares for the people, the pagan sailors, the babies, and even the animals! God even cares for the rebellious, disobedient Jonah.

It is shocking that the man of God's faults are so blatant and exposed. We usually try to hide our faults, as though we would be better than Jonah, as though we do not ever harbor ill will, as though we truly care for people, as though we truly want our enemies to repent rather than to be destroyed by God's wrath. We want to hide that part of our lives just like we want to avoid the fourth chapter of Jonah. What Jonah needed is exactly what we need: God's grace! We, Jonah, Nineveh, and the sailors all need the same thing: more of God's amazing grace.

Conclusion

In Matthew 12:41, Jesus says, "The men of Nineveh will stand up at the judgment with this generation and condemn it; for they repented at the preaching of

Jonah, and now something greater than Jonah is here." God wants us to repent and be saved, and he sent Jesus to preach to us. "The Lord is not slack concerning His promise, as some count slackness, but is longsuffering toward us, not willing that any should perish but that all should come to repentance" (2 Pet 3:9).

God wants us to be saved. He wants the entire world to be saved, and he uses everything he has to make that happen.

> For God so loved the world that He gave His only begotten Son, that whoever believes in Him should not perish but have everlasting life. For God did not send His Son into the world to condemn the world, but that the world through Him might be saved. (John 3:16–17)

Jesus really does love us, and the Bible really does tell us so.

That's the story of Jonah. God uses everything at his disposal to save people. He used a storm to save the sailors, and a fish and a worm to save Jonah. Shockingly, he was able to use a miserably flawed Jonah to save Nineveh, and more shockingly, he used the death of his son to save us.

Discussion

1. Jonah ends with a question. What is the answer, and why is not included in the book?
2. Jesus compares himself to Jonah. What similarities and dissimilarities do you see in Jesus and Jonah? And who they preach to? (Matt 12:41)
3. Peter's father's name is often translated as John. Why would Jesus call Peter "The son of Jonah?" (Matt 16:17, John 1:42 What correlations in the lives and personalities of Jonah and Peter do you see? (John 21:15–17)
4. Where can you see grace in the story of Jonah?
5. Compare Jonah's grace with God's grace. Which are we more like?
6. Can you see a comparison between the book of Jonah and the full story of the prodigal son?

7. **THE GRACE OPPORTUNITY**
TODD JOHNSTON

MATTHEW 18:21–35

One Main Thing

God's grace opens up the opportunity for us to conduct lives of grace directed at others.

Introduction

I don't care much for ultimatums. Ultimatums make me uncomfortable because they force me to make life altering decisions. It appears to some that Jesus makes an ultimatum with his words in Matthew 6:14–15.

> For if you forgive others their trespasses, your heavenly Father will also forgive you, but if you do not forgive others their trespasses, neither will your Father forgive your trespasses.

When we forgive others, God forgives us. When we do not forgive others ... well, God does not forgive us. Of all the extremes in the Bible, this might be the most difficult. It isn't difficult because I don't desire to obey Christ; I deeply desire to obey Christ, but the difficulty comes because I know how hard it is to forgive others. More times than I care to admit I do not want to forgive those who wrong me. But I know that I must forgive, and ultimately, I want to want to forgive. I find myself in the same conundrum as Paul in Romans 7:19. What I want to do I don't do.

Going Deeper

I believe the mistake comes from perspective. The Gospel of Matthew repeatedly mentions the heart of the true believer. The most impactful occurrence is of Jesus himself in Matthew 15:8–20. Jesus references Isaiah 29:13 to show the impact of the heart problem among the law-abiding traditionalist of the day. These individuals, much like traditional extremists of today, are so blinded by their tradition that they refuse to open their hearts up to love that only comes from Jesus. Jesus says it best, "So for the sake of your tradition you have made void the word of God" (Matt 15:6). Heart problems inherently cause perspective issues. When the heart is not focused on the love of God and love of others (Matt 22:36–40) the Christian will fail in living like Christ. The perspective, thwarted by the heart problem, is where the mistake comes. Often Matthew 6:14–15 is read with a "what can God do for me" selfishness. This causes the view that what Jesus spoke is an ultimatum. Think for a moment what might happen to our perspective if the scripture was read instead as, "What can I do for God and His people?" This completely changes the interpretation! Instead of looking at what we can GET, we look at what we can GIVE. This is the perspective, the heart, that we must have. This is the thought process that allows us to set our minds according to the Spirit instead of the flesh (Rom 8:5). This is what Jesus spoke of in encouraging his followers to find a greater blessing in giving than receiving (Acts 20:35) and is certainly what he was referencing to the sons of Zebedee (James and John) in Matthew 20:26–28 where he speaks to servanthood being greatest. When we have a give and not get perspective, we see Jesus's words in Matthew 6:14–15 not as an ultimatum but as an opportunity to provide forgiveness and grace. The availability to receive forgiveness and the ability to give it is at the very heart of Christianity. If we desire to live like, be like, and act like Christ we must have forgiveness at the forefront of our minds.

Later in Matthew's Gospel, Jesus offers a parable to drive the point home, the Parable of the Unforgiving Servant (Matt 18:21–35). To properly understand this text, we must first review the immediate context. In verses 15–20, Jesus discusses conflict resolution. We often look to this passage for "permission" to disfellowship wayward brethren. However, we see the main theme of both these passages in Peter's response, "Lord how often will my brother sin against me, and I forgive him? As many as seven times?" (v. 21). Both passages concern forgiveness and the mindset that one must have to offer it.

Peter understood the rabbinic tradition of the day, as did Jesus, which said that if you forgive a man three times you are not obligated to forgive him a fourth.[1] So when Peter offers the rhetorical seven, he believes he is extending great quantitative mercy. However, Jesus is not looking for quantitative mercy, but qualitative mercy. This is seen in his response, "I do not say to you seven times, but seventy-seven times" (v. 22). That's how the ESV and some other translations render the verse. We might be more accustomed to the KJV's "seventy times seven," which we calculate out to be 490. Of course, any calculation misses the point that what Jesus intends to communicate to Peter is that you cannot set a number on how often we offer forgiveness, just as we would not want God to set such a number for the forgiveness we enjoy. So there is no need to calculate using first century common core here; Jesus is simply implying that forgiveness is limitless, and grace never ends. He illustrates with a parable.

A powerful king has a servant who owes 10,000 talents. This was an unimaginable size of debt. The talent was the highest unit of currency, and a debt of

10,000 talents would have been astronomical.[2] This number is so large a sum that it would be impossible for the servant to ever pay the amount back in his lifetime. The number may possibly represent "more than the entire annual income of the king, and perhaps more than all the actual coinage in circulation in most kingdoms ... at that time!"[3] Perhaps the incomprehensible number finds itself hardly even equated with the forgiveness graciously given to us by God.

When the servant comes before the king he asks for patience and promises he will repay the debt. The king, knowing better, not only offers the patience, but he forgives the debt completely. This is the story of God we live each day. I am reminded of the hymn "He Paid a Debt He Did Not Owe."

> He paid a debt He did not owe.
>> I owed a debt I could not pay
>>
>> ...
>>
>> And now I sing a brand-new song,
>> Amazing Grace [all day long].[4]

How awesome would the story have been if it had just ended here. The master has patience, the servant is forgiven, grace is applied and not denied. But this is not just a story about the victory of grace God supplies; it is a story about our need to apply the same grace to others.

With his slate of debt erased, the servant walks

joyfully to his next appointment. He calls a fellow servant who owes him a hundred denarii. This would equate to a hundred days' wages,[5] a minuscule amount compared to that which the forgiven servant owed. Now this is the part of the story we all see coming or at least we think. Of course, the newly forgiven servant will forgive his servant! Right? Then Jesus throws in the twist. The indebted servant asks for patience, just like the forgiven servant had done to his master, but not only does this forgiven servant fail to provide patience, but his greed and ruthlessness drives him away from the principle of grace and instead to vengeance. The forgiven servant imprisons the indebted servant until he can pay the debt.

Bystanders respond shocked and began spreading the news. The king found out, summoned the forgiven servant, and revoked his forgiveness due to the servant's unwillingness to show mercy and grace.

Application

There appears to be a sort of succession in receiving and applying forgiveness and grace. There is a request for forgiveness, a reward offered by grace, and the required response of the forgiven to forgive others just as they had been forgiven. It is an opportunity and not an ultimatum. The teaching of the parable is a calling for Christians to forgive. We forgive because God has forgiven us even when we could not pay. He asks that we impart grace as it has been imparted to us. Can we really call ourselves followers of Jesus Christ if we do not forgive like he forgives?

This can make us extremely uncomfortable! And this discomfort can drive us to be self-proclaimed theologians asking questions like, "Does this mean our salvation is dependent upon our actions instead of God's grace?" But this is folly. Salvation is imparted by grace through faith (Eph 2:8–9), and this living faith drives us to desire to do good works (Jas 2:14–26). After all, this is what we were created for (Eph 2:10). Jesus is plain and practical. Do not expect your greater sins to be forgiven if you are not willing to forgive others.

The deeper we go into this idea of forgiveness the harder it can become. The greater the relationship the greater the chance for hurt and need for forgiveness. It is one thing to forgive a colleague for not inviting you to a birthday party, but it is something entirely different to forgive the husband who commits adultery, the neighbor who sexually assaults your daughter, the person who murders your wife, and so on. Intimacy provides the opportunity for greater loss and makes grace and forgiveness more difficult. The need to forgive is greater than ever, but we simply do not know how, and quite frankly, we don't want to. This is where it will take a providential act of the grace God supplies.

We see the real-life account of this parable in Paul's letter to Philemon. Onesimus is a runaway bondservant deserving of punishment. Paul, though, asks

Philemon to have mercy, patience, grace, and forgiveness toward Onesimus. He even says, "receive him as you would receive me" (v. 17). The message of Philemon is reconciliation and partnership. This is a vision of grace! Philemon receives Paul's words not as an ultimatum, but as an opportunity to provide forgiveness and grace.

Corrie Ten Boom recounts her vision of grace in her book *The Hiding Place*. Corrie Ten Boom was a Dutch Christian and Holocaust survivor who was placed in a Nazi concentration camp for protecting Jews from the Gestapo. She recounts speaking at a church in Germany about forgiveness after the war. After she finished speaking and stepped down from the pulpit she noticed a familiar face walking towards her. It was one of the chief guards from the concentration camp where she and her sister were incarcerated. This man was the culprit who beat her sister mercilessly resulting in her death not many days later. As he walked straight toward Ms. Ten Boom he reached out his hand and said, "Oh, Fraulein [ma'am], how grateful I am for your powerful message. To think that Jesus washed my sins away." Corrie Ten Boom found herself paralyzed with fear and anger. She later wrote these words,

Even as the vengeful thoughts boiled through me, I saw the sin of them ... and yet I could do nothing about it. I could not feel even the slightest spark of love or charity. And so, I breathed this silent prayer. "Jesus, I cannot forgive him, please give me your forgiveness."

And with that prayer she was able to lift her hand from her side and touched the hand of the man who had persecuted her.

From my shoulder" she writes, "along my arm and through my hand passed a current from me to him ... and in that moment I discovered that it is not on our forgiveness any more than on our goodness that the world's healing depends, the world's healing depends upon God. When our Lord tells us to love our enemies, he gives us, along with the command to do it, the love itself.[6]

To forgive is not an act of your will power, but it is a divine function of grace. It means you make a conscious choice to move forward, unbound by evil. Jesus isn't making an ultimatum when he says we must forgive in order to be forgiven. Instead I believe he is providing an opportunity for how, we too, can provide visions of grace in the lives of our neighbor just as God has done for us. On Corrie Ten Boom's tombstone it is inscribed, "Jesus is Victor." Is Jesus your victor? May our hearts be forever changed to apply what God provides.

Grace: unmerited favor. A gift I simply do not deserve.

Discussion

1. What must we do to change our hearts and minds to look more like Jesus?
2. Jesus says we must love one another (John 13:34), but do we have to like each other?
3. What are ways God has had grace on your life?
4. Are there traditions we have today that make it difficult to show the love of Christ? Should we get rid of some traditions? Should we keep some?
5. Paul said he was the chief of sinners (1 Tim 1:15). Should we view ourselves in this way? Does viewing ourselves as sinners contradict the grace God gives us?
6. The king forgave the servant and later revoked that forgiveness because he was unwilling to forgive his servant. It appears that the king forgave, but did not forget. Does God forgive and forget? Does he forgive but not forget? Can we be forgiven today, but lose that if we stray from Him tomorrow? When we forgive must we forget?

Endnotes

1. W. C. Allen, *The Gospel According to Saint Matthew*, The International Critical Commentary (Edinburgh: T.& T. Clark, 1912).

2. R.T. France, *Matthew: An Introduction and Commentary*, Vol. 1 (Downers Grove, IL: InterVarsity Press, 1985).

3. Craig S. Keener, *The IVP Bible Background Commentary: New Testament* (Downers Grove, IL: IVP Academic: An Imprint of InterVarsity Press, 2014).

4. "He Paid a Debt He Did Not Owe," *Praise for the Lord,* John P. Wiegand, ed. (Nashville, TN: Praise Press, 1992), 859.

5. Keener, *The IVP Bible Background Commentary: New Testament.*

6. Corrie Ten Boom, John L. Sherrill, Elizabeth Sherrill, *The Hiding Place* (Westwood, N.J., Barbour, 1971), 238.

8. **WHEN GRACE APPEARED**
W. KIRK BROTHERS

JOHN 1:17–18; Titus 2:11–14

One Main Thing

Grace is "favor bestowed when wrath is owed" (Jack Cottrell). God gave a new definition of grace through the life and death of Jesus Christ.

Introduction

The world can never be the same once it has been introduced to a Plato, Beethoven, Vincent van Gogh, Florence Nightingale, Abraham Lincoln, Marie Curie, Amelia Earhart, C.S. Lewis, Alexander Graham Bell, Rosa Parks, Michael Jordan, Bill Gates, or Elvis Presley. Certain individuals introduce the world to thoughts, feelings, sights, concepts, beauty, ministries, scientific discoveries, and technologies that transform life. No human being has changed the world the way Jesus, the Son of God, has. One area in which he brought change was in our understanding of grace.

Going Deeper

In the Old Testament, the main Hebrew word for "showing grace/favor" is *ḥānan*. About this word, Jack Cottrell notes that it "seems to be God's favorable attitude that moves him to bless and answer prayer."[1] In the New Testament, the Greek noun often translated "grace" is *charis*, which can have a variety of definitions, ranging from "grace" to "gratitude" to "generosity" to "beauty." But in Jesus Christ, God reveals realms of grace unanticipated by such definitions.

John 1 focuses on who Jesus is (God, Creator, man, Lamb of God who takes away the sins of the world, etc.). Though he is co-Creator of all that is (vv. 1–4), he became a human being ("flesh") and "lived among us" (v. 14). He brought the glory of God to earth and was "full of grace and truth." The term translated "full" (*pleres*) can have the idea of "all that it will hold," or, on the other hand, "complete" in the sense of "lacking nothing."[2] John 1:17 says, "For the Law was given through Moses; grace and truth were realized through Jesus Christ." While the general idea of favor/grace was present in the Old Testament, we need to remember that this favor could be based on someone's worthiness. In contrast, as Jesus, who is "full" of grace (1:14), came and showed us the Father (cf. John 1:18), we saw a new concept of grace. In John 1:16, John the apostle described Jesus has having "grace upon grace." The idea is a continual supply of grace. When one supply of grace ends, another comes ... "grace upon grace." The one who is full of grace and brings a never-ending supply of grace, shows us what true grace is.

The apostle, Paul, referred to the coming of Jesus as "when grace appeared" (Titus 2:11). Verses 11–14 form one long sentence in Greek. In the preceding section, Paul has described what healthy teaching and living looks like for older men, older women, younger women, younger men, and slaves (2:1–10). "For" at the beginning of verse 11 ties the following verses back to the preceding. He is giving the reasons for why Titus should teach these things and all Christians should practice them. Paul accomplished this by focusing on two "appearings" (Titus 2:11–15). One is the appearing of grace. This refers to the first coming of Jesus (when Jesus "became flesh"; John 1:14). This appearing of grace brought salvation to humanity (Titus 2:11). This was only made possible because Jesus "gave himself for us to redeem us" (2:14).

This phrase can serve to turn our attention to God's definition of grace. We noted earlier that Jesus brought a new understanding of grace. What is this new under-standing? Remember that in the Greek culture, *charis* referred to favor bestowed on another and could have the idea that this favor was unforced or uncoerced. The grace of God, which appeared with the coming and death of Jesus, is a more intense grace than that which was seen in the Greek culture. God's grace was not just unforced favor, but it was also undeserved favor. In fact, Paul says that Jesus, the one undeserving of death, gave his life to save us, the ones undeserving of life. Jack Cottrell notes,

> Such words as unmerited, unworthy, and undeserved do apply to the concept of grace, but they are not really strong enough to reveal the full extremity of grace. The fact is that grace is not merely undeserved or unmerited; it is the very opposite of what is deserved or merited. We are not just unworthy of God's forgiveness; we are actually worthy of its opposite.[3]

In light of this, Cottrell defines grace as "favor bestowed when wrath is owed." This is my favorite definition of grace. God gave salvation to people who deserved destruction, freedom to individuals who deserved imprisonment, and life to sinners who deserved death. This was a richer and deeper definition of grace than existed in the Greek culture. The divine definition of grace was not found in a Greek lexicon, it was found in the life and death of Jesus Christ.

Application

Paul told Titus that the coming of grace not only brought something (salvation), it taught something (sensible living). It taught humanity to "deny ungodliness and worldly desires and to live sensibly, righteously, and godly, in the present age" (Titus 2:12). The word translated as "instructing" in verse 12, is *paideúo*. It means "to provide instruction for informed and responsible living." The "fullness of grace" which we see in Jesus also teaches us how to live. If grace is favor bestowed upon us in spite of what we deserve based on our actions, we might conclude that our actions do not matter at all. This would be a false assumption (cf. Rom 6:1–2). My goodness can never earn salvation. This is because I am not good. Paul told the Roman Christians, "There is none righteous, no not one" (Rom 3:10). Though my actions cannot earn God's grace, they always flow from it. Titus 2:14 tells us that Jesus came not only to redeem us, but to purify us. He did not just come to save us but to sanctify us. Sanctification is the process of becoming holy, of becoming like Christ (cf. 2 Cor 3:18). Those touched by God's grace should seek to live righteously every day. As Jesus came to earth to reveal God and the fullness of grace, so we should live to display God and grace in our lives.

Conclusion

Paul also tells Titus that as we live the righteous lives that the coming of grace has taught us to live, we are able to look with confident expectation toward the second appearing that is mentioned in Titus 2, the appearing of glory (2:14). When he comes in glory, those of us who have accepted his grace will share in his glory. This is in stark contrast to Hebrews 10:27, which describes those who continue to sin willfully without repentance after having received a knowledge of truth. They have a "terrifying expectation of judgment." The Christian is able to live looking up, to live looking forward to the moment Christ returns. I have often said, "I live for the levitation." First Thessalonians 4 says we will meet him in the air at the second coming (the appearing of glory). I live and long for that moment when my feet will leave the ground. In that moment I will know that all my worries are over. That is one of the gifts that grace gives us. When grace appeared, the hope of glory appeared. This hope can buoy us in our darkest hours of trial. Paul says that the appearing of grace brought salvation, the hope of the appearing of glory brings us strength, and the result should be a life of godliness. May we accept his grace, live his grace, and look expectantly for the ultimate gift of his grace, sharing his glory.

Discussion

1. Describe someone who entered your life and taught you something that changed you forever.
2. How is God's concept of grace in Christ different from what we see in the Old Testament?
3. How is God's concept of grace in Christ different from what we see in the Greek culture?
4. What do you think it means to live "sensibly"?
5. What is the most valuable thing you have learned from this lesson?

Endnotes

1. Jack Cottrell, *God: The Redeemer*, What the Bible Says Series (Joplin, MO: College Press, 1987), 364.

2. Frederick W. Danker, et al., *Greek-English Lexicon of the New Testament and Other Early Christian Literature* (3rd ed.; Chicago: University of Chicago Press, 2000), 826–27.

3. Cottrell, *God: The Redeemer*, 376.

9.   **GRACE IN THE GUTTER**
ARVY DUPUY

JOHN 8:1–11

One Main Thing

No matter where we are, Jesus meets us there and offers us grace.

Introduction

In Albanian it is hir; in Italian it is *grazia*; *gracia* is the Spanish word; and in Welsh it is *gras*. Of the over seven thousand languages spoken today they all have a word for grace. And in every language it is a powerful word. It has been said that freedom or love are the most powerful words in the world. As believers we would say that grace tops them all. Because grace is the demonstration of God's love to humanity and through grace we can experience freedom. The New Testament is full of grace language. One amazing account is found in John 8:1–11. Twelfth-century scholar Eustathios of Thessaloniki called it a "great pearl of the gospel."[1] It is a priceless account of a costly gift.

Going Deeper

Palestinian women in the time of Christ lived a hard and heavy life. They were marginalized by the general culture. They were further ostracized in Judaism via a blatant disregard of Jewish law. They did not survive unless connected to a man in some way. Society of that day was patriarchal, and here men are driving this woman to her execution. With all of this in mind it stands to reason that this woman's treatment, throughout this ordeal, would have been less than gentle. You can imagine her being dragged through the streets of the city; pushed, jerked and man-handled, literally. She is then brought to a very public place, likely the Court of the Women in the temple. This woman, whose testimony was not accepted in a court of law, was now having a host of witnesses use her to pass judgement on our Lord.

She was caught in the act which indicates this mob, or at least some of them, were witnesses to the event. The man is conveniently absent from this scene. Leviticus 20:10 says both are guilty. From the onset we see that this was never about truth but about treachery.

The mob wanted to catch Jesus and the woman was the bait.

The horde of holier-than-thou men had already assumed all the roles in this kangaroo court: witnesses, arresting officers, prosecuting attorneys, judge, jury, and they were standing at the ready to play the part of the executioner.

With the snare in place and all things at the ready, they asked Jesus what he thought. What Jesus says is always important but in addition to his words in this narrative, his stance communicates much as well. When the crowd approaches Jesus, he is seated; however, when they pose the question, he does the exact opposite of what we might think: he stoops instead of standing. Why? We cannot say definitively. However, could it be that although he had been questioned by the crowd, he was more interested in the one caught?

If we return to our consideration of how the woman was treated through this ordeal, how do we envision her "placement" at the end when they arrive at their destination? Do you think she was given a seat? Or allowed to find her own place? At least one translation does say she "was made to stand before the group." However most translations say they "set" or "placed" her in the middle. Knowing the culture, the situation, and mob mentality, it is difficult to think this was in any way a gentle process. It is logical to conclude that she was thrown to the ground when she was dragged in by the mob. This means that when Jesus stooped he put himself at eye level with the woman. In this moment of chaos—public arena, class interrupted, mob with his destruction as their agenda—Jesus focused on the woman. John R. Stott said that grace is love that cares and stoops. Philippians 2:7 tells us he set aside the privileges of deity and took on humanity; that is a long way down. His entire life and ministry was one big stoop, and he carried it through all the way to the cross. After kneeling down the mob presses him even more. Finally, he stands up and speaks, but he says very little in the later part of verse 7. Then verse 8 tells us he kneels once more. The words of Jesus penetrate the hearts of those comprising the mass and they leave. They slip out of the Court of Women and back to their lives, hopefully changed because of their encounter with The Master. Jesus then stands up again and asks the woman where her accusers are. In this moment he seeks not information—he knew they were gone—but recognition from the woman, recognition that although they had tried to destroy her and him, they could not.

Application

The question, where are your accusers, is still relevant today. We all have people in our lives that will not let us live down a moment, an event, a word. They are always there to try and remind, reignite, and reinjure.

Maybe our worst accuser is ourselves, constantly reliving the past, rehashing a mistake, or reliving a poor choice. Just like with this woman, our accusations are always with us. We long for relief, but it will not come in this age. That is because of who is behind the accusations. Satan is identified as the accuser in Zechariah 3. He loves to get us and keep us prisoners of our past. We all have things in our past we wish we could redo, but we cannot, and we do not have to because of Jesus. Satan's favorite tool in his toolbox is guilt. But the blood of Jesus washes all that away.

So if you are struggling with that, this text is for you. It is preserved through the ages not only to show what Jesus did on that day but to show what Jesus does today. The Christ who saw her and put himself where she was will do that for us today. He sees us, regardless of where we are, and he loves us. And today he defends us. He is with the Father in heaven defending us against the one who accuses us daily. We must let the defense of Christ silence the slurs of the devil. We are not who we used to be before we came to Jesus. As Paul wrote "I have been crucified with Christ and I no longer live, but Christ lives in me. The life I live in the body, I live by faith in the Son of God, who loved me and gave himself for me" (Gal 2:20).

When we come to Christ, he moves us to a place of grace, he reclaims his rightful territory. Juan Carlos Ortiz said that watching a trapeze show is breathtaking. We wonder at the dexterity and timing. We gasp at near-misses. In most cases, there is a net underneath. When they fall, they jump up and bounce back to the trapeze. In Christ, we live on the trapeze. What happens when we slip? The net is surely there. The blood of our Lord, Jesus Christ, has provided forgiveness for all our trespasses. Both the net and the ability to stay on the trapeze are works of God's grace. Of course, we cannot be continually sleeping on the net. If that is the case, I doubt whether that person is a trapezes artist or not.[2]

Just like the woman, our Lord offers his grace to us when we least deserve it. When this transpires the acceptance of such grace should move us to another place in our lives. Not that we will never sin again but that through prayer, study, and focused living we will sin less frequently, and when we do we will recognize it and repent of it more quickly.

In the end, we are left with many questions. However, there is one certainty that is beyond doubt. This woman experienced what every human longs for today: a second chance. This teaching has been used and abused through ages. It has been and is used as proof text of for opinions and arguments of a broad variety. Beyond all the arguments, this text is a powerful demonstration and testament to why Jesus came—to pick us up out of the dirt of our sins and give us an opportunity for a real life.

Discussion

1. What do you think happened to the woman
   from this moment on? How was her life
   different?
2. What do you think happened to the
   members of the mob? Were their lives
   changed because of what happened here?
3. What do you think those were listening to
   Jesus teach when the mob appeared
   understood and took away from this event?
4. If you had to describe the grace of God,
   what one word would you use?

Endnotes

1. Quoted by Jennifer Knust, "The Woman Caught in Adultery (John 8.1–11)," Bible Odyssey,

   https://www.bibleodyssey.org/en/passages/main-articles/woman-caught-in-adultery (accessed April 4, 2019).

   2. Juan Carlos Ortiz, *Living With Jesus Today* (s.l.: Creation House, 1982), 160.

10. **GRACE IN THE BOOK OF ROMANS**

MICHAEL JACKSON

ROMANS 3:21–24

One Main Thing

The grace of God, embodied in the death of Christ on the cross, demands a response from believers. The gift is surely free and cannot (could not) be earned through meritorious work. But grace compels the Christian to a new way of living, Christ having defeated sin victoriously on the cross.

Introduction

The word "grace" occurs in the New American Standard version of Romans 21 times in 18 verses, but the concept undergirds almost all of Paul's thinking throughout the entire letter. Paul's explanation of the gospel in Romans is centered by his own personal understanding of God's grace (Rom 1:5). He had first received it himself, and now he has rethought everything in light of his own personal transformation.

From Paul's consistent opening formula in 1:7 ("Grace to you and peace from God our Father and the Lord Jesus Christ") through his closing doxology in 16:20 ("The grace of our Lord Jesus be with you"), his letter to the church situated in Rome is stamped from front to back with thoughts of grace. This is consistent with Paul's conversion and his understanding of God. Where would Paul have been without God's intervention on the road to Damascus? He says later in 1 Corinthians that it is "by the grace of God, I am what I am" (15:10).

This deeply personal understanding of grace stands behind Paul's exposition of God's rescue of the human race through the Messiah Jesus. Paul knew what it was like to be under sin, falling short of the glory of God (3:23). He knew what it was like to miss the all-to-important message of Jesus and his teachings. And he later knew what kind of peace with God comes as a result of being reconciled with God (5:1 and 5:10). Paul understood his teachings about the Messiah from his expansive knowledge of Old Testament Scripture. But he also understood his teachings from the very distinct and personal point of view of an apostle who was "untimely born" (1 Cor 15:8).

Paul felt that this grace which he knew from his study and his experience had real and practical implications for the way he should now live. In Romans 1:14 he will say that he is "under obligation" to preach the gospel to anyone who will listen, presumably because of what God has done for him. This "obligation of grace," we might call it, is an important theological point for Paul in all of his letters, but particularly in Romans. Paul was evidently slandered by others for teaching about God's grace, because they misunderstood him to be teaching that people could do evil because God is so gracious (3:8). A critical point of the letter to the Romans is 6:2, where Paul definitively states, "How shall we who died to sin still live in it!" God's grace is good and efficacious, but it is no reason to dive headlong into sin.

This is so important to Paul that he speaks of two "reigns" over the human race: the "reign" of sin, and the "reign" of grace (5:21). We'll explore these further as we go a little deeper.

Going Deeper

For the reigns of sin and grace to make sense, we must first consider what a reign actually is. The reign of a king or queen is the exercise of sovereign power or rulership over a certain territory. This is the figurative picture we get in the passage at the end of Romans 5— like a king or queen would rule a country, grace now rules the world. But how can that be?

First, we must recognize that sin is real and truly

exercised its own reign or rule over the world from the very beginning (5:12). From the time that man first received a commandment, he broke it. And from that point forward, sin seized its opportunity (see this metaphor for sin in Gen 4:7) in each of us, as we have all made choices to break the commandments of God in one way or another.

The earliest chapters of Romans are the sure way for us to see this. In Romans 1:18–32, we read of God's wrath being poured out on those who sin in rebellion against God. And lest we should be too self-confident in our morality, Paul says in 2:1 "Who do you think you are?" (my paraphrase). What I mean by this is that Paul asks why we would pass judgment on another, because we too have committed sin. Even Jews, who were given the Law, were guilty of trespassing it (2:17–24). So, Paul can confidently say that God is impartial (2:11), and that all have sinned and fall short of his glory (3:23).

When I was 2 years old, and barely putting words together, we had a great big snow storm in our little section of Northwest Alabama. Snow is not common where I was raised, so even a dusting is a great experience that leads flocks of people to the grocery store to purchase bread and milk lest they perish. My parents were extremely excited about the snow, realizing that they would be able to bring their newly minted toddler to the large front window and show him the picturesque scenery of several inches of snow. As they pulled back the curtains, they said I put together my first ever sentence: "What a mess!"

And so it is with sin. A mess! As God has given us direction to follow, we have inevitably stepped outside of what he's asked for us to do and to be. And this has happened with everyone. A mess indeed.

But just as sin had its reign (and with sin comes death, because that's what the payment for sin is according to 6:23), there came along another reign. What could come along and give a proper response to sin? Romans 5:17 is helpful here:

> For if by the transgression of the one, death reigned through the one, much more those who receive the abundance of grace and of the gift of righteousness will reign in life through the One, Jesus Christ.

The Messiah Jesus Christ! God's gift to us of Jesus Christ (3:24) dealt a resounding blow to sin once and for all (Hebrews 9:28). How grateful we should be to God for this!

In our day and time, sin can no longer claim that it holds its reign over the earth (1 Cor 15:56–57). Jesus has claimed that victory, defeating sin and death. Does this mean that we do not all sin and fall short of the glory of God? Unfortunately not. Sin still finds its ways of attack and we all still fall through temptations. But, spiritually speaking, for those who choose to respond to God's gift of grace with belief, repentance, confession, and baptism (Rom 6:3–4), there's a new sheriff in town.

Grace reigns. And the wages of grace are life.

> so that, as sin reigned in death, even so grace would reign through righteousness to eternal life through Jesus Christ our Lord. (Rom 5:21)

Application

This is great news, but what does it mean to the Christian and how the Christian should live? This is the very question Paul raises in Romans 6:1.

> What shall we say then? Are we to continue in sin so that grace may increase?

So many Christians have just this sort of response to the message of God's grace. Since God has conquered sin, and did so even when we were all so bad (helpless, 5:6), why don't we just keep on sinning and let God continue to show up and defeat sin? While many people have treated grace like this, Paul's answer is as strong as any in all of Scripture: "God forbid!" (6:2).

Why is it that those who have responded to God's grace in belief, repentance, confession, and baptism should no longer live in sin? Because God's grace creates in us an obligation (6:14).

When your mom or dad gave you something freely as a gift, did you then go and immediately trade that gift for something else or try to sell it? If you were gifted a new car, would you go and trade it in for your old one? Neither should you or I, as ones who have received the grace of God, exchange it for our old body of sin. Paul says it this way:

> But now having been freed from sin and enslaved to God, you derive your benefit, resulting in sanctification, and the outcome, eternal life. (Rom 6:22)

Conclusion

We all know people who have great gifts and talents in this world, and yet they squander them and waste them. We all know Christians who have been given the beautiful gift of the gospel, and yet do not feel any obligation to it. What sort of response will we give to God's beautiful gift of eternal life that comes through the Messiah Jesus?

Discussion

1. Look up grace in a concordance or Bible app and find all of the occurrences in the

book of Romans. Which verse stands out to you among those listed, and why?

2. How did Paul's personal conversion story influence and impact his ministry? Why?

3. In what ways have you personally seen sin to be a destructive force in this world? How does this relate to God's grace?

4. What is the proper Christian response to God's grace, and why?

5. How does it feel to see someone who has an abundance of blessings, gifts, and/or talents squander them all away? Why do we feel this way to those who make choices like that? How does this relate to the concept of grace?

JEREMY BARRIER

GALATIANS 2:20–21

One Main Thing

God is lovingly making an offer of unmerited, divine favor to humanity. Will we accept or reject the offer of His grace?

Introduction

Jim was standing there at his front door. He was a little disoriented. It was about 8:30 am, and typically his mind wasn't really working yet until his second cup of coffee. However, on this morning, while sipping on his first "cup o' Joe," wearing his favorite pinstripe, navy pajamas, and squinting down at his phone to catch whatever emails had been blitzed to him during the night, suddenly the doorbell rang. So. There he was, standing in his pajamas, cup in one hand, and opening the front door with the other to greet his curious, wide-eyed neighbor. They had been neighbors for about one month now, but they had still not met due to an overly busy life adjustment as Jim had accepted a job offer in a new city, and they had been so busy with the move. Nevertheless, there was the overly-eager neighbor, with a steaming hot cherry pie in hand, and something of a "welcome to the neighborhood!!" exuding from his body.

Jim—never one to be overly hostile, nor on the adverse, overly kind in temperament—was actually a little irritated at having to answer the door at a time of day that seemed a little on the early side. "9:00 am," he thought to himself, "might have been a little better." At any rate, his "better self" was attempting to master his mind, and he gently felt the dimples in the corner of his lips begin to rise and say "hello" with a mild cheerfulness—forced—through his barely open mouth, and tips of his front teeth gleaming whitely. He was demonstrating his social graces as best he could, realizing that his neighbor was trying to say "hello" for the first time.

The question that comes to my mind is: "Jim, would you really reject your neighbor's cherry pie? How rude can you be!" To accept or reject a gift, while many times is not difficult to sort out, it can, in some cases, be more complicated than we would like to admit. In this case, Jim was inconvenienced, but for him to reject the gift ... that would be downright insulting and rude. Not to mention the fact that it would very likely sour the relationship with his neighbor that he probably would have to see on a daily basis!

Going Deeper

As we delve into the subject of grace, it is sometimes astounding to me, how we can begin by making the issue quite complicated, and then try to work our way out of it. At the end of the day, grace is one of those ideas that quite simply focuses on the fact that God loves us and wants to do something nice for us. It is a gift—completely undeserved on our part. In many ways, it is the same as a father who decides to offer his daughter a "slushie" from Sonic on the way home from school. Does my child deserve it? No. Do I want to make her happy? Yes! Do I want to express my love for her in this small act of kindness following a long day at school? Absolutely! At any rate, you get the point. Grace is gifting our love to others. Grace is God gifting his love to us. But better than a "slushie" or a cherry pie, he gave us the gift of his son.

The idea of "grace" is explicitly articulated in Paul's letter to the Galatians. It is not only the dominant theme of the letter holistically, but it shows up in small ways in Paul's words.

Grace be to you and peace from God the Father, and from our Lord Jesus Christ. (Gal 1:3)

I marvel that ye are so soon removed from him that called you into the grace of Christ unto another Gospel. (Gal 1:6)

But when it pleased God, who separated me from my mother's womb, and called me by his grace. (Gal 1:15)

And when James, Cephas, and John, who seemed to be pillars, perceived the grace that was given unto me, they gave to me and Barnabas the right hands of fellowship. (Gal 2:9)

I do not frustrate the grace of God: for if righteousness come by the law, then Christ is dead in vain. (Gal 2:21)

Christ is become of no effect unto you, whosoever of you are justified by the law; ye are fallen from grace." (Gal 5:4)

Brethren, the grace of our Lord Jesus Christ be with your spirit. Amen. (Gal 6:18)

While a quick survey reveals that Paul likes the word in both "heavy" (e.g., Gal 5:4) and "light" (Gal 1:3) settings, it is essentially an expression that deals with God "gifting" certain things to humanity. While I think Paul may whip out the word in his greetings and salutations, he doesn't do so without thought. In other words, if Paul says "I'll be praying for you"—as we so often times say to people in their struggles—Paul would never, ever have said that expression without meaning it deeply.

I say all of this to make a simple point. According to Paul, God is standing at the door, offering the Galatians something far greater than a cherry pie, and they don't have the sense to accept the gift! Of course, if they had understood what God was offering, then, well, it might have been another story.

One of the problems we have in reading Paul's letter is that once we figure out what they were really arguing about—circumcision as a means to attain good standing before God—it seems so bizarre and foreign to us, so that we can easily lose the major point. But we need to understand why circumcision was such a big deal.

Even though circumcision is pretty common in modern America, Christians and non-Christians participate in this minor medical procedure usually without any thought toward religion but because it is a part of our culture. But circumcision had very definite religious and cultural meanings for the Galatian churches. So, the question becomes "why would they feel compelled to circumcise some of their male members, and how could this have been perceived as rejecting the gift (i.e., grace of God)?" These are good questions and they don't have a clear, definitive answer in the text. In other words, Paul's letter gives us the response to a problem, however he doesn't clearly explain to us the circumstances that led to his writing the letter. He mainly hints at the historical context. However, with some thought and close reading, we can probably imagine a situation.

While Paul doesn't unpack the situation that led to the crisis, we know that there most assuredly was a situation and context that brought about Paul needing to write the letter. Consider a few scenarios. First, imagine that one of your loved ones, even your child, becomes deathly sick. What do we usually do in dire situations such as this? We pray. And we start making promises to God! "God, if you will save my child, I promise I'll never skip a service again ... I promise I'll give more ... I promise, I'll stop losing my temper." The list goes on and on. I think something similar was happening in ancient Galatia, but instead of making promises, the Galatian Christians were presented with an alternative avenue to securing the blessing of God. I would imagine that the Galatian churches were facing such challenging situations that they decided that they needed to do more to prove their devotion and faithfulness to God. In other words, their expressions of faith in Jesus Christ that led them to be baptized into Christ ... these were not enough (Gal 3:26–28). They needed to somehow prove their devotion to God. Enter the Jewish ritual of circumcision, the sign of the covenant people of God ever since the days of Abraham (Gen 17).

It is so hard for the Galatians to accept that God's grace is being offered to them, not based on their actions, but based on God's love for them! They cannot accept the fact that they are presentable in the eyes of God, based on their willingness to simply trust and accept God's gift! As Paul says, "I do not frustrate the grace of God: for if righteousness come by the law, then Christ is dead in vain" (Gal 2:21). They were unwilling to accept God's offer of Grace through a simple ritual of baptism. They thought they had to do more, be more, trade more with God to be worthy of it. You see the problem, don't you? We are never worthy to barter with God.

The error they made is understandable. In times of crisis, we not only make promises to God, but we also criticize God too. "God, where are you?" "How could You have let this happen?" In both cases, promises and criticisms, we are essentially going back to the bargaining table with God and saying, "did we not make this agreement clear enough? I thought the deal was, I follow you, and you bless me? Did I not prove my devotion with the first agreement? Are you punishing me now? Have you bailed on me and my loved ones?" This "questioning of our faith" is the natural outcome of adversity. The Galatians were no doubt facing adversity and weren't sure what to do. They were wavering.

Application

Many times, it becomes difficult to see clearly what is going on. We fail to realize the key features of our lives as they relate to God. A summary might be as follows. First, we are not righteous. We mess up. We mess up often. We say things to our spouses that we shouldn't. We fail to act and do what is right, at work, at home, wherever, and people get hurt, because we don't rise to the challenge. Again, we mess up. Second, we fail to realize how overpowering God's love is for his children. God, like a parent, looks down upon his sleeping children at night, and is simply glowing with warmth and love for us as he watches us sleep. We don't take this into consideration. Third, God, in his love, is simply trying to offer a gift to us. We do mess up, God knows it, and God is willing to overlook it. This is grace. This is God's gift. This is God standing at our door and offering to be friends, neighbors, and have a bond, a relationship with us. It is not merited! We don't deserve it! He desires it! Last, but not least, there is simply nothing we can do to make God love us more. He never gave the gift, because it was an 'eye for an eye'. This is not the situation where your neighbor does something for you, so you are going to do something nice to keep the scales balanced. This is not that kind of situation. This is more like coming home from a long week in the hospital after a terrible car accident that you have just been through, and the medical bills are running about $200,000 and you can't pay it! Then, suddenly, your elders show up and say, "the church will pay the bill." You can't pay it back! This is a gift. When you are presented with a situation like this, there is only one appropriate response: say "Thank You!" Realize the situation you are in and simply say "Thank you, God." failed to happen, doubt crept in. John knows that Jesus is the Messiah in Matthew 3. However, by chapter 11 John is having serious doubts spring up because his circumstances did not meet his expectations. It is easy to see why John begins to wonder if Jesus was "The Coming One" as he waits to die in his Roman prison cell. What John expects does not match his reality.

Conclusion

As Jim stood there at his door, initially desiring to be "irritated" for the morning inconvenience, it occurred to him what was happening. He felt guilty for his selfish thoughts. He felt ashamed that his coffee and morning emails had trumped such a kind gesture. As his smile began to grow on his face, he leaned forward, extended his hand, and said, "hello!" "Welcome to my house, neighbor! I don't think we have met yet, but I have been wanting to meet you!" Jim realized that his neighbor was offering him not only a cherry pie but also kindness and friendship. As a clear token of humility, Jim leaned forward, accepted the pie and looked his neighbor in the eye and said with as much heartfelt emotion as he had within him, "thank you. You didn't have to do that, but, thank you so much."

You see, when we decide to make our promises and offers to God service, devotion, or commitment, the real question is whether or not we have first been willing to even acknowledge what God is offering us. Are we even acknowledging his grace? We are indeed justified by our "trust" in God, and not of ourselves or our ability to keep any set of laws or guidelines. Are we willing to accept God's kind gift or are we simply going to reject it?

Discussion

1. What is grace? What does grace look like in our world today? What is God's grace?
2. In Paul's world, the Galatian churches were attempting to practice the ritual of circumcision as a way to "earn" their salvation by "proving" their devotion to God. What are some ways that we might attempt to "earn" our salvation with God?
3. What might lead the Galatians to feel the need to circumcise some of their members? How might this have 'impressed' or "pleased" God?
4. Appreciating God's "grace" is truly a

mindset that we have based on our understanding of what God has done for us! How can we appreciate better God's kindness for us on a daily basis?

12. REMEMBERING WHY
PHILIP GOAD

EPHESIANS 2:1–10

One Main Thing

We preach and teach about **what** seemingly all the time. But being motivated by **why** will ensure that we always stay focused on our purpose!

Introduction

If you have been a Christian for any length of time, perhaps you've experienced a season where your walk with God lost some of its meaning and became an exercise in going through the motions. It's not uncommon, and when meaning goes missing from our Christian walk, it could mean that we are experiencing burnout. Burnout can lead to a reluctance to dive into new ministry opportunities. Or those times when meaning is missing could mean that we've simply lost sight of our purpose.

Further, as we attempt to please God, sermons we hear and Bible classes we attend keep us constantly reminded of what God expects of us. Here's the thing: Even though we fail from time to time, I would contend that most of that time, we know **what** we should be doing. It seems to be more about whether we'll be motivated to live out what we know the Bible teaches! That's why this study on grace is not so much about new information as it is re-motivation! We must constantly be thinking about whether our lives are having the impact that they should in a world that desperately needs what Jesus has asked us to offer.

The big idea for this study can be summed up in this way: We preach and teach about **what** seemingly all the time. But being motivated by **why** will ensure that we always stay focused on our purpose. God's amazing grace should always serve to motivate us!

As we consider Ephesians 2:1–10, we want to consider three motivational questions based on the text. Three questions that can help us remember our why, prevent us from falling into the trap of simply of going through the motions, and get us back on track any time we lose our way.

Going Deeper

Motivational question #1: Has God done enough?

> And you were dead in your trespasses and sins, in which you formerly walked according to the course of this world, according to the prince of the power of the air, of the spirit that is now working in the sons of disobedience. Among them we too all formerly lived in the lusts of our flesh, indulging the desires of the flesh and of the mind, and were by nature children of wrath, even as the rest. But God, being rich in mercy, because of His great love with which He loved us, even when we were dead in our transgressions, made us alive together with Christ (by grace you have been saved), and raised us up with Him, and seated us with Him in the heavenly places in Christ Jesus, so that in the ages to come He might show the surpassing riches of His grace in kindness toward us in Christ Jesus. (Eph 2:1–7)

Paul begins by reminding the Christians at Ephesus, and ultimately us, of our pre-Christian past. He states in v. 1, "You were dead in your trespasses and sins." We were dead spiritually, and it was our fault, not God's. We were buried in our trespasses. God's wrath is what was awaiting us. Verse 4 begins with two amazing words: "But God." God intervened. God made it possible for our eternal ending to be completely different. He made us alive together with Christ. The text states that it wasn't because we were important or deserving. Verse 4 states it was "because of His great love with which He loved us." The idea that God raised Jesus from the dead is amazing. Yet we should also be amazed that God cared enough to raise us too!

And so our question: Has God done enough? I was dead, but now I'm alive. I was destined for wrath, but now I'm on my way to heaven. We should be thankful for his grace every day. Unfortunately, bad circumstances sometimes kill our motivation and cloud our view. Sometimes valleys cause us to forget about our call to service; the idea that we are still here for a very important reason. Sometimes we are so deeply buried in our own garbage that the last thing we can think about is serving someone else in need. Perhaps it's a sickness we didn't expect. Perhaps we've lost a loved one way too soon. Perhaps we are discouraged, because of the person who mistreated us rather than loving us. And during those times, we prayed fervently. We beg for a better tomorrow, but nothing seems to be changing for the better. It's possible to become concerned that God isn't fixing enough of the things that are going wrong in our lives.

But the truth is, according to Ephesians 2, God has already fixed the only thing that really matters. We were dead, and now we are alive. The truth is, God has already done more than enough! The story of the Bible is about all that God has done to fix our sin problem, and that should keep us motivated and ever mindful of our purpose.

Motivational question #2: Has God asked too much?

> For by grace you have been saved through faith; and that not of yourselves, it is the gift of God; 9 not as a result of works, so that no one may boast. (Eph 2:8–9)

Achieving a successful walk with God can be a daunting task; especially in light of all of the commands found in scripture. Think about some of the challenges we face. First, we spend our lives attempting to become more like Jesus, and we should be doing that. However, we also understand that the perfect life that He both lived and taught is actually out of reach for us. Perfection is the goal, but we will always fall short. Second, because we are still human, Christian living often becomes a frustrating process of taking a few steps forward, followed by a failure and a step or two back. Therefore, in one sense, the case could be made that God, has indeed, asked too much! But in those moments of frustration, this text and this motivational question is of great value.

Notice the good news in the text. God hasn't asked too much, because salvation is "not of ourselves." Our obedient faith is necessary, but our obedient faith earns us nothing. Our salvation is God's gift to us. By definition, a gift cannot be earned. So what about all of those commands that we are attempting to obey? We continue to put forth our best effort, because by the grace of God, we are alive spiritually. God could never ask too much of us! We walk in purpose because we are grateful. The next time you are trying to decide whether to dive into a new area of ministry, think about this question and this passage.

Motivational question #3: Is there anyone who isn't worth our best effort?

> For we are His workmanship, created in Christ Jesus
> for good works, which God prepared beforehand so
> that we would walk in them. (Eph 2:10)

God raised us for a reason. We were dead. Now we're alive! And God's purpose is now supposed to be embraced by each of us. Verse 10 reminds us that we are His workmanship. It further teaches that we have been created in Christ Jesus for the purpose of walking in good works that God has prepared for us. But how often do we fall into the trap of living like some people just aren't worth our best effort? What about our families? Sometimes we treat strangers better than the people we love the most. What about our co-workers? We may be spending as many waking hours with co-workers as we do with family? Do the people at work deserve to see our best effort at a faithful walk with God? What about that person that serves us at our favorite diner three times a week? And then what about the irritants in our lives? Few of us would admit to having enemies but most of us have people in our lives who just rub us the wrong way. Do they deserve to see our best effort?

Objectively, we know that everyone is worthy of our best effort. We grew up singing "Jesus loves the little children; all the children of the world." We're constantly mindful of the truth contained in John 3:16, the idea that God so loved "the world." We think about Genesis 1:26 where we are taught that man is created in the image of God; the only part of the creation to receive that designation.

It's undeniable. The Bible teaches us that every person is worthy of our best effort. But the question is, is our **why** big enough to cause us to take **what** we know and put it into action? These things are easy to talk about but difficult to live out, especially in those moments when we are delayed, mistreated or otherwise inconvenienced.

Application

Why is all of this so important? It's because of our purpose. Most of us interact with "dead" people every day—people who, according to Paul, are still dead in trespasses and sins (Eph. 2:1). The grace of God has provided us with salvation. Woe to us if we neglect to interact with people in a way that would help them want what we have.

Notice one more big idea from Paul, a mindset that will help guarantee better success for us as we attempt to walk in purpose. In Acts 20, Paul is concluding a final face-to-face visit with the elders at Ephesus. They are about to pray, embrace, and shed tears, because they believe they will not see Paul again on this side of eternity (vv. 36–37). It seems that everyone must be leaning in, hanging on every one of Paul's words. And in that highly emotional moment, notice what he says in verse 24.

> But I do not consider my life of any account as dear to myself, so that I may finish my course and the ministry which I received from the Lord Jesus, to testify solemnly of the gospel of the grace of God.

Paul says, "It's not about me!" And that mindset is still our key to success today. Take a moment to imagine with me: What would your church family look like if every family member became a little bit better of living this out? Would it be easier to stay focused on **why** and to walk in purpose? Would your church family be able to make an even bigger difference in your community? Would embracing Paul's mindset result in more souls being added to the population of heaven?

Conclusion

We can picture in our minds what could happen if every member could remember these three motivational questions and Paul's powerful advice. However, the real question is, are we all willing to change enough to allow that picture to become the shared reality?

Comedian Michael Jr. said the following: "When you know your **why**, your **what** has more impact because you are walking in or towards your purpose." As a blessed recipient of the grace of God, are you walking in purpose today?

Discussion

1. What motivates you to serve God?
2. What causes you to lose motivation in your Christian life? What negative consequences do you see at those times?
3. Do you wish that God would be more active in your life? How do you deal with those feelings?
4. What motivates you to serve people whom you do not like?

13. MY GRACE IS SUFFICIENT
BRAD MCKINNON

2 Corinthians 12:1–10

One Main Thing

An inflated sense of self-importance is incompatible with the Christian faith. Rather, as disciples of Christ, we should rely on God's grace to keep us humble during good times and inspire us in more challenging circumstances.

Introduction

Relationships can be tricky to navigate, and Paul's association with the Corinthians was certainly complicated. Paul first visited the important commercial city of Corinth during his second missionary journey (see Acts 18). His time in Corinth included meeting Aquila and Priscilla, a husband-wife ministry team, who would become two of Paul's dearest friends. They worked together as tentmakers,[2] while Paul participated in synagogue discussions every sabbath. He found some evangelistic success, with Crispus a synagogue official (among others) becoming a believer in Jesus as the Messiah. But Paul faced opposition, too. He was brought before Gallio, the proconsul of Achaia, although he was released after a brief hearing. After staying a "considerable time" in Corinth, Paul returned to Antioch leaving a new group of believers behind—a group that included mostly those who lacked education, power, status, and wealth (1 Cor 1:26–28).

These new converts faced ethical, theological, and social challenges. These tests served as the basis for a series of letters and visits between Paul and the Corinthians that likely took place over a few years. These interactions included (1) our letter of 1 Corinthians, (2) an earlier letter that Paul had written (cf. 1 Cor 5:9), (3) a letter or letters that the Corinthians addressed to Paul (cf. 1 Cor 7:1), (4) a "painful visit" Paul made to Corinth (2 Cor 2:1), and (5) another letter written by Paul "with many tears" (2 Cor 2:4). Many scholars believe 2 Corinthians to be a composite of several letters with chapters. 10–13 constituting this "sorrowful letter" mentioned in 2 Corinthians 2.

By the time of the writing of the last section of 2 Corinthians, several issues had developed that strained the relationship between Paul and the Corinthians. Earlier, an individual had publicly opposed Paul, but that issue had been rectified (2:5–11). In addition, the Corinthians felt insulted, because Paul did not accept financial assistance from them, as he did other churches (12:13). And a group of rivals had emerged that Paul mockingly described as "super-apostles" (12:11). They claimed Paul's "letters [were] weighty and strong, but his bodily presence [was] weak, and his speech contemptible" (10:10). These opponents boasted of their apostolic credentials over against Paul's, and Paul worried that his relationship with the Corinthians was in danger of slipping away.[3]

Paul responded to his critics by listing some of his own sufferings for the cause of Christ (11:21b–33). Then, however, it's as if Paul catches himself in midsentence, and concludes "nothing is to be gained by [boasting]." He then proceeds to tell a strange story about an out-of-body experience and a "thorn in the flesh" that had taught him some important lessons: (1) boasting about your own self-importance is foolish; and (2) there is great value in relying on God's grace. God's grace can humble you when you're feeling a little too proud of yourself, and it can lift you up when you're struggling.

Going Deeper

Even though Paul claims to see no profit in boasting about himself, he claims he must go on to discuss "visions and revelations of the Lord" (12:1). This may serve as a rhetorical device: "I don't want to brag, but if

I have to because of my opponents, then I have an impeccable resume that they can't touch." Paul's credentials include a direct relationship with Christ. Paul tells a story about "a person in Christ." Referring to himself in the third person adds dramatic effect. It denotes sarcasm, while also leaving the impression of humility. This experience was evidently a major event in Paul's life, because he remembers the exact year ("fourteen years ago"), but he's also intentionally fuzzy on the details ("in the body or out of the body I do not know").

Paul explains that he was caught up to the third heaven (the significance of the distinction in the numbers of heavens here is unclear) or Paradise (12:2, 4). Paul's description of his own apotheosis[4] is intended to place him not in the place of God, but in close proximity to God. Paul knows his place. He understands he's a mortal and acknowledges there are some things permissible to utter and some things that aren't. He doesn't want to establish his own personality cult, although he certainly could have done so. To guarantee Paul's humility, "a thorn was given [him] in the flesh." He describes this "thorn" sarcastically as a gift or messenger of Satan. There's no real value in trying to fill in the gaps of Paul's story to determine what this "thorn of the flesh" was; it evidently is something that manifested itself physically that brought some sort of pain or humiliation to Paul.

In Scripture, as well as in Jewish and Christian

traditions, Satan operates only in the realm of God's permission. In other words, the Satan can only do what God allows him to do. So, Paul appeals to the Lord three times to have the source of pain or weakness removed. The Lord's refusal to remove the impediment is presented in benevolent terms: "My grace is sufficient for you" (12:9). Thus, we learn that the kingdom of God operates on different terms than typical earthly structures. For Paul, weakness is a gift, because it allows him to act ("power") in ways that allow him to experience the way of Christ in all its fullness ("perfect").

Application

There are two extremes when it comes to one's spiritual mentality. One you might define as egotism—an exaggeration of your own importance. The other is self-scorn. The problem with both extremes is that they accept what some have called "a Jesus-plus theology." On the one hand, someone might think, "I'm so important, have so many gifts, and offer such precise obedience that the will of God can't possibly be done on earth without me." Another might conclude, "I have so many challenges the Lord couldn't possibly use me to do the will of God on earth." Paul's excursus at the end of 2 Corinthians disputes both of these possible scenarios. No one is indispensable, but neither is anyone beyond reach. God's grace is sufficient.

This realization has the potential to affect positively how we interact with each other in our homes, churches, and communities. If we reject arrogant pride and completely surrender to God, we are better situated to welcome everyone as worthy of love, because God's grace is sufficient. If we endure humiliation as Christ did, we are better prepared to understand our own utter dependence on God, because God's grace is sufficient.

Conclusion

There is a local homeless ministry in our community that uses the tagline, "Everyone Matters." If everyone matters, then no one is more important than another.

All of us have gifts that we can use to share in what God is doing in this world, because God's grace is sufficient to remake this world into something that resembles God's kingdom. If everyone matters, then no one is less important than another. All of us have challenges that can remind us to remain humble, realizing that this is God's work and not our own. This notion is expressed well by C.S. Lewis in *Mere Christianity*: "[The Christian] does not think God will love us because we are good, but that God will make us good because He loves us."[5]

Discussion

1. How does Paul's complicated relationship with the Corinthians underscore the value of God's grace?
2. Describe a time in your life when you felt like weakness was a blessing instead of a curse.
3. List ways that worldly institutions rely on power to function. How do these ` assumptions differ from an understanding power in the kingdom of God?
4. In what ways would rejecting arrogance and pride enhance family, church, and community relationships?
5. What practical steps can your local church take to support the "everyone matters" ideal?

Endnotes

1. The following resources were particularly helpful to me in developing this study: Frederick W. Danker's *II Corinthians* (Augsburg Commentary on the New Testament, 1989), Sze-kar Wan's introduction to 2 Corinthians in *The New Oxford Annotated Bible: New Revised Standard Version with the Apocrypha* (Oxford University Press, 2010), and *Paul for Everyone: 2*

Corinthians (Westminster John Knox, 2004) by N.T. Wright.

2. The term translated "tentmakers" may indicate those who work with leather or canvas to fashion temporary structures used for dwellings or even theater props (see Frederick W. Danker, et al., *Greek-English Lexicon of the New Testament and Other Early Christian Literature* (3rd ed.; Chicago: University of Chicago Press, 2000), 928–929).

3. Fortunately, Titus arrived with good news for Paul concerning the Corinthians' faith (2 Cor 7:13–16).

4. The term "apotheosis" refers to the assimilation of a human person to a god. This notion was prominent in the ancient Greco-Roman world. See *The Concise Oxford Dictionary of the Christian Church* (Oxford University Press, 2nd ed., 2006), 33.

5. C.S. Lewis, *Mere Christianity* (New York: Scribner, 1952), 49.

BIBLIOGRAPHY

Allen, W. C. *The Gospel According to Saint Matthew*. The International Critical Commentary. Edinburgh: T.& T. Clark, 1912.

Berlin, Adele. *Poetics and Interpretation of Biblical Narrative*. Sheffield: Almond, 1883.

Bush, Frederic W. *Ruth, Esther*. Word Biblical Commentary 9. Dallas: Word, 1996.

Cottrell, Jack. *God: The Redeemer*. What the Bible Says Series. Joplin, MO: College Press, 1987.

Danker, Frederick W., ed. *Greek-English Lexicon of the New Testament and Other Early Christian Literature*. 3rd ed. Chicago: University of Chicago Press, 2000.

Danker, Frederick W. *II Corinthians.* Augsburg Commentary on the New Testament, Minneapolis, MN: Augsburg, 1989.

France, R.T. *Matthew: An Introduction and Commentary*. Tyndale New Testament Commentaries. Downers Grove, IL: InterVarsity Press, 1985.

"He Paid a Debt He Did Not Owe." *Praise for The Lord*. John P. Wiegand, ed. Nashville, TN: Praise Press, 1992.

Keener, Craig S. *The IVP Bible Background Commentary: New Testament*. Downers Grove, IL: IVP Academic, 2014.

Knust, Jennifer. "The Woman Caught in Adultery (John 8:1–11)." Bible Odyssey.
    https://www.bibleodyssey.org/en/passages/main-articles/woman-caught-in-adultery (accessed April 4, 2019).

Lewis, C.S. *Mere Christianity*. New York: Scribner, 1952.

Livingstone, E. A., ed. *The Concise Oxford Dictionary of the Christian Church*. 2nd ed. New York: Oxford University Press, 2006.

Nielsen, Kirsten. *Ruth*, Old Testament Library. Louisville: Westminster, 1997.

Ortiz, Juan Carlos. *Living With Jesus Today*. s.l.: Creation House, 1982.

Peterson, Eugene H. *Five Smooth Stones for Pastoral Work*. Grand Rapids: Eerdmans, 1980.

Prinsloo, W. S. "The Theology of the Book of Ruth." *Vetus Testamentum* 30 (1980): 330–341.

Rauber, D. F. "Literary Values in the Bible: The Book of Ruth." *Journal of Biblical Literature* 89 (1970): 27–37.

Sakenfeld, Katharine Doob. *Ruth*. Interpretation. Louisville: John Knox, 1999.

Ten Boom, Corrie, John L. Sherrill, and Elizabeth Sherrill, *The Hiding Place*. Westwood, N.J., Barbour, 1971.

von Rad, Gerhard. *Old Testament Theology*. 2 vols. New York: Harper & Row, 1965.

Wan, Sze-kar. "Introduction to 2 Corinthians." Page 2025 in *The New Oxford Annotated Bible: New Revised Standard Version with the Apocrypha*. New York: Oxford University Press, 2010.

Wright, N. T. *2 Corinthians*. Paul for Everyone. Louisville, KY: Westminster John Knox, 2004.

Younger, K. Lawson. *Judges/Ruth*. The NIV Application Commentary. Grand Rapids: Zondervan, 2002.

11:2	48
11:3–4	47–48
11:6–7	48
11:8–9	48
13:14	41

Joel

2:13	41

Amos

1:1	43
7:12–15	43

Jonah

1	54, 56
1–3	54
2	55–56
3	55–56
3:4	43, 55
4	54
4:2	41

Micah

4:10	41

Zechariah

3	83

Malachi

New Testament

Matthew

3	102
6:14–15	61, 63
11	102
12:41	58, 60
15:6	62
15:8–20	62
16:17	60
18:15–20	63
18:21	64
18:21–35	61, 63
18:22	64
20:26–28	63
22:36–40	62
25	10
25:1–13	11

Mark

8:27–33	49

Luke

1:30	3
2:52	3
15:20	49

John

1:1–4	73
1:14	73–74
1:16	74
1:17	73
1:17–18	72
1:18	74
1:42	60
3:16	111
3:16–17	59
8:1–11	79–80
8:7	82
8:8	82
13:34	70
21:15–17	60

Acts

2:39	27
7:46	3
9:16	50
18	114
20	112
20:24	112
20:35	63
20:36–37	112

Romans

CONTRIBUTORS

Bill Bagents (DMin Amridge University) is Professor of Ministry, Counseling and Biblical Studies at Heritage Christian University.

Jeremy Barrier (PhD Brite Divinity School, Texas Christian University) is Professor of Biblical Literature at Heritage Christian University.

W. Kirk Brothers (PhD Southern Baptist Theological Seminary) is President of Heritage Christian University.

Nathan Daily (PhD Claremont Graduate University) is Heritage Christian University Registrar and Assistant Professor of Religion.

Robin Dunaway (BA Heritage Christian University) is a missionary to Southeast Asia and South America.

Arvy Dupuy (MA Amridge University) is Adjunct Instructor at Heritage Christian University.

Ed Gallagher (PhD Hebrew Union College) is Professor of Christian Scripture at Heritage Christian University.

Philip Goad (MMin in progress Heritage Christian University) preaches for North Highlands Church of Christ in Russellville, Alabama and serves as Director of Alumni Relations at Heritage Christian University.

Travis Harmon (MMin Heritage Christian University) is Vice President of Student Services and Instructor of Ministry at Heritage Christian University.

Matt Heupel (MMin Freed-Hardeman University) is Adjunct Instructor at Heritage Christian University and preaches for the Woodlawn Church of Christ in Florence, Alabama.

Michael Jackson (EdD Union University) is Vice President for Academic Affairs and Associate Professor of Education and New Testament at Heritage Christian University.

Todd Johnston (MDiv in progress Heritage Christian University) is minister for the Thomaston Road Church of Christ in Macon, Georgia.

C. Wayne Kilpatrick (MAR Harding School of Theology) is Emeritus Professor of Church History at Heritage Christian University.

Brad McKinnon (PhD in progress Aberdeen University) is Associate Professor and Director of Field Education at Heritage Christian University.

To see full catalog of Heritage Christian University Press and its imprint Cypress Publications, visit www. hcu.edu/publications.

www.ingramcontent.com/pod-product-compliance
Lightning Source LLC
Chambersburg PA
CBHW061733050726
47598CB00002B/460